# The Best Kept Secret Is "You"

### A Journey into the Rabbit Hole with Autism and Love

By

## Daniel James Wilson

Strategic Book Publishing and Rights Co.

Strategic Book Publishing and Rights Co.
12620 FM 1960, Suite A4-507
Houston TX 77065
www.sbpra.com

ISBN: 978-1-62212-372-8

The author of this book does not dispense medical advice or prescribe the
use of any technique as a form of treatment for physical or medical
problems without the advice of a physician, either directly or indirectly.
The intent of the author is only to offer information of a general nature to
help in your quest for emotional and spiritual well-being. In the event you
use any of the information in the book for yourself, which is your
constitutional right, the author and the publisher assume no responsibility
for your actions.

"One out of 110 children is determined autistic."
—2010

# Contents

# In Gratitude

To Martha, for your undying support and understanding, for giving birth to our three beautiful children even after all the major trials of the first experience, and especially for allowing me to stay in the midst of some of your most vulnerable times in life. Expressing in words doesn't really show the appreciation I have for your incredible being.

To Daniel, for your constant teachings, especially your love. I am forever grateful for your gift. Only the equipment is broken; I see your soul.

To James and Mary, for your giving and understanding in all the chaos and trials with your brother and parents. I am grateful for your steadfast stubbornness to get my attention and for knowing what you needed for yourselves while in the midst of caring for your brother.

To my mother, who reminds me that our minds, our thoughts, affect who we are.

To my father, for being an active participant in allowing me to question who my real father is, and for allowing me to see that he is human.

To my grandfather, for always being there and for accepting, supporting, and understanding without judgment. You are all the things I aspire to be. You made sure my three brothers and I were taken care of by always offering nutritional meals that consisted of soda pop, fried chicken, and candy.

To Joe, your place is the perfect setting for writing, silence, rabbits, and owls.

To Ann, for believing in me and for helping me see that I am more than "just a roofer." Your questions – do you love yourself; what is your son's gift to you – comments – you didn't do anything wrong – and your inspiration and guidance to write this book, and all your support helped me finish this book!

And to "You," I hope this helps to remind you of what you already know!

# Epigraph

*"Love the Lord thy God with all thy heart, all thy mind, all thy soul, and all thy strength. The second most, love thy neighbor as thyself. On these two commandments, hang all the law and the prophets."*
—Jesus, The Bible, King James Version

*"The Buddha said this, 'The object of your practice should first of all be yourself. Your love for other, your ability to love another person, depends on your ability to love yourself.'"*
—John McQuiston II

*"As for all the handicapped, only the equipment is not functioning, the 'Being' is there!"*
— Daniel James Wilson

*"Love is without question, just as you are without the question!"*
—Daniel James Wilson

# Snowflake

Be like a snowflake,
Shaped in your own perfect way,
Different from everyone else,
Dancing in the sky.
Landing gently with others.
Melting, becoming one with everyone else,
Forming a stream providing
Brilliant-colored water for life!

As I've come to know me, I now see Daniel.
That is all he needed.
We can't know others if we don't know our soul.
When do we stop hiding our essence!

# Preface

Throughout my early life, I suffered in silence, and the depth didn't show until 1979, when I observed my son's heart-wrenching birth and watched helplessly as my bewildered wife endured excruciating pain. Later, I listened to a doctor label my son *autistic*. What the hell is autistic? Back then, I had never heard the phrase *developmental, neural disorder*. Not having any experience, I relied on the doctors' authority and professionalism. I depended on them for answers, and still there was no meaningful support or information of which I could take advantage. I knew there was something divinely special and real about my son, and that kept me inspired and motivated; I would not accept that there was nothing I could do to help him. Also, the guesses and misinformation that I had to endure were unacceptable, yet I had to keep silent for fear of causing more issues for my speechless son.

Looking back, I had no other choice. I had to walk a fine line. I was resigned to the fact that my son could easily be abused by the system. Not knowing what autism was made me feel helpless. That, coupled with no one to talk with, made it unbearable at times. My son's unconditional love and joy made me question any doubt I had. His unbelievable acceptance of love and our bond have made a powerful impact on my life. How could I leave him? How could I even think of leaving him and Martha, his mother, without support? What would happen to them if I died? Who would take care of them? I knew I had to stay—my son kept me alive!

Still, I was tired of my life, tired of doing the same thing day in and day out. I felt done and ready to die. A roofer by trade, I'd frequently say to myself, *So, what if I fall off the roof? Dig me a hole, and shove me in, and I'll be a happy camper.* Many times, I wished I would fall. I was just a roofer. Would anyone even notice? How long would it be before someone would even notice? Many times, I wanted to be done with this life. All these thoughts and questions wandered in silence through my mind every day of the year, along with the anticipation of wrestling matches every evening with my son. I'd leave my home in Bakersfield at the crack of dawn, and in winter, it was still dark. I'd drive for a couple of hours to work on a roof all day in the hot sun—and sometimes, even in the snow—and then I'd drive back only to continue working at home, repairing the parts of the house that my son would've destroyed in fits of rage.

Though my gut told me that it wasn't my fault, I still kept blaming myself and asking the same questions over and over: Why did this happen to my son? Why did this happen to us? What did I do wrong? What am I doing wrong? What is wrong with me for thinking all these thoughts about dying? One day, I finally heard a response!

For the first time, I felt seen and heard. I met someone named Ann, who told me that I didn't do anything wrong and there was a gift in my son's situation. Before that time, I didn't know what I now know about this "gift." I felt I really didn't have a choice except to die, but Ann taught me instead to take a journey into my past, and I realized that the answers I was seeking were all within me. I discovered that emotions are our most direct link to our souls and to our abilities to feel and to know.

Up until then, I hadn't realized that I had been a person who was numb, shut down, and unconscious. I had been sleepwalking throughout my life. For years, I did not allow myself to emote. It's only been recently that I realized my emotions are real and must be expressed because they are the part of me that engages with what I really know—my intuition, what I am feeling and sensing. I realized that, when I suppress my emotions, I am not only denying my self-expression, but I am denying others permission to experience their feelings and be who they are. When I'm not transparent with others, I'm not only cheating myself; I am cheating others of my truth. This self-expression is what makes us unique individuals.

Emotions engage us in love, compassion, and many other feelings that we've had since birth. What we do with these emotions determines how we respond or react to situations. Usually, when we are triggered, we react to something that has already happened, such as an old experience that is resurfacing in thought. That's when we either shut down, flee, fight, or freeze. I have been known to mostly shut down and flee when triggered. Now, I have learned that, by embracing and acknowledging my feelings and expressing those emotions through writing or by speaking to someone else, I am being true to myself and free to live a fulfilled life of understanding, compassion, and love.

Please keep in mind while reading this that this was a new start for me. The past has now ended. Ann suggested I write a book about my son after I connected with him for the first time in 29 ½ years. After all these years, I now reflect on how I love myself and my son, and in this reflection, through seeing myself, I saw him.

As you read, you will see that, in 2010, I woke up screaming. You will see the story seems to leave my son, as I could not see him for who he was. In other words, the more I knew my thoughts, the more I saw my son and my friend. Now, in this time, I have found that, through expressing these things with others, this "seeing" is not confined to my son only, as you may see if you allow yourself to read all that follows.

# Chapter 1

Ann said, "You can't die yet! You have a story to write!"

Those words stopped me in my tracks, and my initial response was, "I don't even like to read. I hate paperwork and never liked homework or writing. I'm not a writer! Besides, what would I write about, and where would I start?"

Ann responded with, "What about the gift of autism, and the relationship between you and your son, and the effects on your family?"

That resonated! I began to write, and the words flowed through me without me thinking about them. I didn't know where these words came from—perhaps from God or a higher source. I didn't question it, so I labeled this voice *God*. I stayed open to what came and wrote it down. I had no idea where I'd be led, and then I realized that it didn't matter. What I knew for sure was that we are twofold beings—one of flesh and reasoning, which I equate to fear, and the other of soul and knowing, which is love. Before, I had never given love or fear a thought, and as I continued to write, I realized that there is something powerful in these two pieces, so down the rabbit hole I went.

I begin here with my own story, my childhood and young adult years.

I've always been curious about many things, especially about how things work. I took things apart and sometimes put them back together again, though not too often. Being raised in a small, three-bedroom house with three brothers wasn't easy, especially as we got older. I shared a room with my younger brother. My two older brothers had their own room. My mother had her hands full with four boys, and at the end of the day, she was often exhausted and would sit in a recliner to rest. Then, my father would arrive home from work, walk through the door, and stop to look around. He'd notice that the house was in shambles and complain that nothing had been done. I'd stand back and observe as my mother remained silent, letting him rant and rave at her. She never argued back, always staying quiet. Many nights, I lay in bed afraid of what my father might do. I was concerned for my life. My father stood tall at six feet, two inches, and since I was just a little tyke, he seemed huge in stature.

After we'd all go to bed, I'd hear my father continue to rant and rave until the glow of his cigarette would pass my room and continue down the hallway. I would then breathe a sigh of relief, knowing that he was done for the night. I remember only one spanking from my father, and that was because my little brother and I lit a fire in the middle of our room to stay warm. Otherwise, my mother kept my father from punishing us. I can also remember camping—not so much the play but the baths in the washtub and the soapy washcloth that burned my ears when my mother scrubbed them. There were times I'd lie in my sleeping bag looking at the stars and think how nice it would be to be up there. In silence, I observed the chaos and confusion around me and tried to understand what was happening while keeping it all to myself. I watched and listened, not saying a word, because I was afraid that, if I spoke up, I would be hurt in some way. I seemed always to be afraid. My father had a volatile temper and snapped at a moment's notice. On one occasion, he took us to P.O.P., an amusement park on the coast. He and my older brothers wanted to ride a large roller coaster, and I was still quite young and scared to death about joining them. Crying, I said I did not want to get on, and my father became hard necked and made me ride it anyway. Since then, I have tried to ride different roller coasters to put that fear behind me without success. But, there was also part of my dad that seemed kind and caring. One afternoon, I was playing in a gully with my brothers when we somehow disturbed a huge beehive in a tree. Out flew a swarm of bees. My brothers ran out of the gully and left me behind, running around screaming. A short time later, my father came and carried me out.

When my parents finally separated, I stood sobbing in the driveway as my father drove off, pulling a silver teardrop camper trailer. I must have been five or six years old. After that, the memories of my father are limited to Christmas visits because those were the only times I saw him. The first time he came back to pick us up, I remember vividly that he and my mother fought physically. He pushed her into a closet by the front door then made us get into his car. My father and brothers discussed the scratches on his neck as I sat quietly in the backseat between my two brothers, wondering what would happen next. I was afraid of his unpredictable behavior and bad temper but remained quiet.

I figured out in my later years that I had assumed many things about my father's behavior during childhood, believing them to be true and blaming myself. The personal issues he was dealing with left him frustrated, confused, and angry, and he did not realize the impact he had on those around him.

When my mother began dating, she would drop us off at people's houses. I was a little boy, barely high enough to look over the kitchen sink, when I was first left in a stranger's home. Left washing dishes, standing on a stool. I watched as my mother drove away in our station wagon. My mom and three brothers and I either slept in that station wagon or stayed at strangers' houses. I recall staying alone with a few strangers and especially remember this very tall albino man who was very loud. I was very scared and confused, and I wondered when my mother would return or even if she would. People always seemed so large to me. Maybe that is why I stoop down to engage with kids today. Most of the time, when my mother would drop me off at places, I would enter the house frightened, almost blacking out, and not remembering anything. On many occasions, my mother introduced me as her little girl because she had expected a girl when I was born. This made me shrink back—I felt humiliated and embarrassed—and fostered an environment that allowed many others to mistreat me. Unlike my brothers, I was a good kid and always wanted to do the "right" thing. I was taunted enough, and I did go along from time to time to fit in because I felt I was a disappointment to my mother. I was very sensitive and emotional and known as a pansy. Because I was this way, my father would say, "He is not my son." Every so often, his words were thrown in my face. I was in a family where I didn't fit and always felt alone and confused. I'd sometimes question whether I really had a different father than my brothers.

Other than the bond I shared with my little brother, I don't recall feeling love for or being loved by anyone except by my maternal grandfather. I did feel he was authentic in his caring, kindness, and gentle understanding. I had huge admiration for him. Like my grandfather, I became involved in the church, where I felt comfortable. I resonated with the Bible studies as if I already knew the material. That led me to reading the whole Bible a few times when I got older.

I was a good student in school. I attended classes every day and did what was asked of me. I excelled in math but was slow in reading even though I tried very hard. I even had tutors and special classes to help me improve. School was difficult on many levels. My mother couldn't afford new clothes for us, so I had to wear holey pants and T-shirts to school, and then I was made fun of by the other kids.

Our mother worked for the phone company and still couldn't afford a sitter to watch us during the summer. So, she would drop my little brother and me off at the Boys Club in downtown Los Angeles. We'd escape to

Griffith Park Observatory in Hollywood; I can't remember how we got home. On one of our walk's I recall my little brother feeling down, and I watched as he jumped over a pipe rail on the high bridge over a wash. He said he was done with his life. He said he no longer wanted to live and was going to jump. I thought he was joking; I told him he was jerking my chain and started to walk away. He started to crouch down as though he was really going to jump. Truly frightened, yelling and crying, I ran back and convinced him to climb back over the rail. By then we were both crying then, and we continued on.

On other days we walked for miles, sometimes dropping in on our grandfather, who would feed us M&Ms, Kentucky fried chicken, and Coke. He gave us designated drawers in his workshop and encouraged us to create things. Those were the good old days. My grandfather was a God-fearing man who attended church on Sundays, ate fish on Fridays, and was very calm in his demeanor. Unlike my father, he always had a great sense of humor.

I was always curious about my grandfather's profession as an electrician. I could usually figure things out, except for electricity, which was invisible and elusive to me. He knew I had an interest and gave me books to study. There was something very special about this man that couldn't be seen, only felt. I started attending church services, though I didn't attend church with him.

While I'm on the topic of church, allow me to share some thoughts. I've always questioned things—as a kid and as an adult. I felt good when attending church services, but then one day, I decided that the hypocrisy was intolerable, so I quit going. Stepping out of the services and listening to people judge, criticize, and complain, I realized that I could stay home and watch services on TV or sit and read the Bible. I didn't quit but felt a deep difference between how the minister lived his life and how the people attending lived their lives. Believe me, I still take good looks at myself and question the purpose of church. I even sat with two different pastors from two different churches and asked for clarification of God's Word and further perspective on some topics while I was researching this book.

As a teenager, approximately 15½ years old, sitting on a bench in high school, I was contemplating my future. I was failing in school and couldn't see myself getting out anytime soon. I remember thinking that it was crazy to continue. In that moment, I decided I would quit and find a job. That decision didn't go over well with anyone else, and I was called to the principal's office along with my mother. The principal commented to me, "You seem to be a smart young man, what seems to be your problem?" That led to nothing but frustration and tears, and I lashed out at them both. I didn't know any better. He wasn't helping, and neither was she.

I was washing dishes at home at 16 years of age when my mother called me a lazy good-for-nothing. I snapped at her for the first time ever and called her names, something I never believed I would do. Even with all my mother's craziness, I still loved her. On that day, I guess, I finally released all the frustration that was building up for so many years. I was shocked with my behavior toward my mother. She went ballistic and threw me out of the house. I moved in with her ex-boyfriend, who was my first boss. He was a roofer. He taught me everything I needed to know about roofing, and that was where my long, labored career started.

During that time, I worked and saved up enough money to purchase a pellet gun. One day, while I was out shooting with a buddy, I watched a sparrow land in a eucalyptus tree. I glanced over at my buddy and said, "Watch this!" I took aim, shot the sparrow, and then went over to see it. I found it on the ground. It was still alive and gasping for air. I watched it breathing, and in that moment, I felt it as myself. I broke into tears and finished him off. I had taken away its life and freedom. I have not shot a thing sense.

After that incident, I met a beautiful, young lady who became my girlfriend. As things progressed, approximately one year later, I moved in with her and her parents in Northridge, California. I was in love, and I expected we would be together forever. She was a sweet and loving gal, and I knew I'd marry her someday. I remember my first attempt at having sex with her. As things got hotter, I broke into tears and told her I could not do it. I had placed myself in her shoes and realized what could happen to her if I followed through. This was soon to be remedied as her parents took her down for birth control pill's.

I realized I needed a good career, so I joined the Air Force expecting to go into electronics and flying. In boot camp, I was told I'd have to wait at least a year before I could fly, so I stayed with electronics. During the second part of technical school, I received a Dear John letter from my girlfriend. I was devastated and thought I'd drown myself. The thought of living my life without her was overwhelming, and I began to drink heavily to hide my sorrow. I was heartbroken! I couldn't wait to go home. While before this, I'd stayed away from fighting, as I didn't want to hurt anyone, I changed my tune.

A couple of months later, full of trepidation, I headed for home in Southern California. In the first week of Christmas break (1977), I picked up my things from my ex-girlfriend's house. I struggled with our last visit and found it hard to move on—I still loved her. The following week, while partying with my brother, he introduced me to his wife's sister. We instantly fell in love. Rebound? Maybe. Unfortunately, I had to return to Mississippi to continue my duties. Fortunately, she was open to my phone calls, and we talked every chance we could get. After two weeks, in a phone conversation, I asked her to marry me. She said, "Yes!" Even though she thought this could be a rebound, it didn't matter to me. I wanted to marry this girl. So, I took time off in March and returned to Southern California for the wedding. Two days later, I returned to Mississippi and thought, *What the hell did I do?*

I didn't even know this woman, let alone love her. I was terrified, confused, guilty, ashamed, and embarrassed at my behavior—and of realizing that this really was a rebound relationship. I am a man of my word and knew that I'd have to honor my commitment. After a few months, I left the Air Force and returned home to be with my new wife.

Instead of going straight to her, I moved in with my mother and pondered what to do. In my mother's straightforward way, she asked, "What is your wife doing in Sacramento? Why isn't she down here with you?" Still not knowing what love was but understanding my obligation, I asked my wife to move from her hometown. We lived with my mother for a short time until we rented our own place. About a year and a half later, we were expecting our first child. I was full of joy about becoming a father, yet fearful of how I would provide for my family and what kind of father I would be. Would I love this child? Could I love this child? I worried about so many things. Money was tight, and having a child was a huge responsibility. Was I ready for this? Was I ready to be a father? I had to trust that all would go well.

We lived in Los Angeles County next to a busy freeway, and we were always dreaming of where we could go in the future. During the pregnancy, my wife ate healthy foods and did not drink alcohol, nor did she smoke cigarettes. She had regular checkups, and the doctor would always say, "Everything is fine. Everything looks good." To us, everything did appear to be going well.

It was a hot summer evening (August 1979), and the time had come. We were eager and anxious when we arrived at the Hospital for check-in. As the time got closer, the doctor was nowhere to be found. I became extremely anxious and thought, *My wife is having a baby! She is having contractions, and the baby is ready to come. Where in hell is the doctor?* The nurses appeared to be nervous but were handling the situation. A nurse asked my wife to hold her pushes until the doctor arrived. I was stunned and full of confusion. I thought, *This isn't what I was taught in classes. Why is this happening?* I trusted the staff even though I felt something was wrong. At regular intervals, the nurses would come in and check the monitors. Finally, a nurse read the printout, then abruptly tore it off the monitor, and said, "Shit!" She threw it into the trash can without looking at either one of us. Again, I trusted the nurses yet felt a tremendous fear coming from the staff and from within. I thought, *A big mistake is happening. What can I do?*

The doctor finally showed up. It was about time! He came into the birthing room where my wife was still holding the baby back as requested by the nurses. When he asked her to push, she didn't have it in her. Her body no longer responded; it was as if she were numb. The urge to push was gone. There was no movement coming from the baby or from her body. I immediately felt there was something wrong. In silence, I kept asking, *What the hell is going on here? My wife and baby are in danger.* At that moment, there was no question about whether I loved her or not. My compassion and duty stepped in to fulfill my obligation to her and now to my new son.

The nurses jumped right in and began and to knead her belly, using forces to push the baby out. Shocked and with disbelief, I watched what looked like hands working dough with four rolling pins. About 19 hours later, my wife gave birth to an eight-pound, seven-ounce baby boy. My son was totally covered in what look like pea soup. He was not breathing or crying! The doctor immediately turned him upside down and suctioned the slimy green matter out of him. Then the nurses took him out of the room abruptly. Unfortunately, what was supposed to be a natural childbirth and a joyous moment turned into a frightening and desperately confusing set of events filled with uncertainty. The question loomed, *Is my son alive?* Fortunately, a short while later, the nurses brought our son back into the room. He was pink in color, with a head shaped like a football, and breathing. This was such a tremendous relief to us all! We named him Daniel.

For those of you who are not familiar with the presence of "pea soup" during delivery, it is a sure sign of fetal distress. This is something I was not taught during natural birthing classes. Of course, in those days (1979), I assume most parents didn't know about fetal distress unless they had experienced it. My experience was not like the movies when babies come out pink and crying. This had been a horrible nightmare!

In roughly two weeks, my son started projectile vomiting but had noticeable weight gain. The doctor still told us, "Everything is fine." Again, I put all my trust in the doctor. My wife, in the same period of time, developed an infection along with depression. Then, after a couple of months passed, Daniel began showing signs that did not appear normal. Little things like clapping our hands wouldn't cause a reaction in him, yet I'd stand next to him, and he would react to a whisper. Like any parent, I began to worry about what was going on. I didn't know what to do, who to call, or where to get answers. The doctors were surely not helping.

At three months, Daniel had an ear infection, and the doctors assumed that his difficulty in hearing was due to fluid in his ears. Within five months, he was scheduled for PE tubes. We agreed to go ahead with the procedure, not knowing what it entailed. It turned out that he would have to be wrapped in a child straitjacket and held down. While sitting in the waiting room, I heard him constantly screaming and could hardly bear it. He was extremely upset. I sat there feeling helpless and frightened. Again, I trusted the doctors and staff. Finally, one of the nurses asked one of us to go in and comfort him. When I entered the room, my son was red-faced, screaming, and wrapped so tightly that he couldn't move. There were at least three nurses and a couple of doctors dressed in white coats standing over my tiny, little guy. What a nightmare to watch this happening! Imagine what my son must've been thinking. I immediately told the doctors to stop and to forget the procedure at this time. The doctors and nurses appeared to be put off, but I didn't care. I couldn't stand to watch my child being tortured in that manner.

Meanwhile, my wife went into a deep depression, and her infection took a couple of months to heal. I was at a loss and full of confusion. We went on short trips to visit relatives to help my wife cope with this distressing time. I hoped this would help her come out of the depression. I was fearful, and I didn't know how to help. Was I doing enough, or was there something else I should be doing? These thoughts totally consumed me. I was completely frustrated and felt helpless with the situation. I kept asking myself, *What am I doing wrong?* The biggest questions that loomed were these: Are my wife and child going to be okay? How could I not love her and the boy?

# Chapter 2

How did the doctors know that everything was fine? What did they know, if anything? How could they keep telling us that everything was fine? In retrospect, I feel they really didn't know and did not know what to say or do.

At six months, the pediatrician told my wife that her breast milk was too fattening, and that was the cause for Daniel's weight gain. But, with her mother's intuition, she knew he would be healthier with breast-feeding, so she continued.

Daniel began crawling at 10 months with his head tilted to one side. He would follow lines on the sidewalk and always look at other lines with his head tilted. He rolled and threw a ball like any other child his age, but when he would stand up, he would collapse. His speech began at a normal age, and he seemed to be progressing. At about 18 months, Daniel was speaking three-word sentences, but at two years, his speech began to deteriorate. At this point, a new behavior began. He would put his hand in his mouth and bang his head gently on different objects. This was disturbing to me. I was curious as to what was going on within him, not to mention wondering if he was hurting himself.

Keep in mind that, all this time, my wife was going to doctors for answers —and it was a pretty good list of doctors by now—with no solid information. Working for a company with health benefits was a big plus, but it still wasn't enough to pay all the bills. I was struggling for advancement in my company, and when I say struggling, I mean I was desperate! I was angry with myself, feeling like a complete failure in supporting my family, and I was scared. I wanted to run and knew I couldn't give up on my wife and son. I always reminded myself of what she must be going through. My wife struggled to get answers, so she sought some kind of support group. We both continued to struggle individually in our own ways to find answers, and then we would come together to exchange information. And still, there was an underlying desperation that was splitting us apart. I kept reminding myself of the commitment to my marriage and now my child. Keeping my commitment and caring for my family was of the utmost importance.

When I'd go home, my wife would share all that had happened during her day, including different observations about our son's behavior, the doctor's information or noninformation, conversations with friends, and finally, the conclusions reached from all these discussions. She'd tell me what she felt we needed to do next, and being a guy whose job it was to be big and strong, I would put my feelings aside and support her in any way I could. I felt it would be selfish of me to burden her with my feelings of inadequacy. I would suggest things based on the information I got from her and my own observations, and then I would hear a rebuttal. How could a man know more than a woman about her child? So, I'd shut up and let her handle the situation.

The frustrations, anxieties, and questions grew about whether Daniel would outgrow this unfortunate condition. I also questioned whether the doctors knew what they were doing. Could they have done something differently? What about genetics? What did we do wrong? My wife and I would look at each other. I'd say nothing and yet feel a great deal. Was it guilt? Then, all the questions started in my mind. I'd question whether I should change jobs. On the one hand, we'd lose benefits, and on the other, I'd make more money to pay all the bills and provide more income for our needs. My hopes for a healthy, happy family were beginning to crumble. The air was thick at home.

I began to notice that my son's head banging was getting progressively worse and wondered what was affecting him. Maybe he sensed all the tension and trouble at home. Did he know what was going on? Was he in pain? Was his eyesight the problem?

I thought I was giving him a lot of love and attention, and still it did not seem to matter. What was he telling me? What did he need? Was I neglecting him because I couldn't understand what he needed or what he was thinking? Was I really seeing him? Could I feel what he was saying without words? What about the love between us? There were so many questions and worries. It was hard to cope with at times.

# Chapter 3

In April 1982, my wife was in labor for almost 10 hours, and finally, my second son was born without any difficulties. James came out naturally pink in color and cried out almost immediately as he was placed into his mother's arms. We visited with tremendous joy until the nurse took him away. His was a good example of a "natural" birth! I was grateful that it went more simply than Daniel's. Upon bringing James home, I saw a glimpse of Daniel's calm as he held his brother in his lap. He gazed at him and stroked his hair. He then leaned over and kissed him—love at its best! Still, I was very anxious and fearful as I watched, not knowing if Daniel would accidentally or purposely hurt his brother. Although I wanted Daniel the hold his brother for hours, I was never relaxed because I never knew when his mood might shift. There were many moments when I wasn't sure how Daniel would behave, so I kept a close watch. I was always afraid that Daniel might bang his head against his brother. But he never did. He never hurt his brother. I now wonder how much fear I projected onto Daniel.

While all this was taking place, there was an even greater need to support my wife. She was now caring for two children and still dealing with doctors who were holding back information. Who would give us straight answers? We never knew what to think as we were always told that doctors know everything. We relied on them for the right information. I found myself always asking, "What's up, Doc?"

I wished I could do more for my wife, but what could I do? I knew she needed more support, especially now with new baby James. So, we talked about moving to Kern County to be near her family. That might help the situation.

I took a few days off work and went to Kern County to look for a new position. I stayed with my wife's family and managed to find two jobs. So, we pulled up stakes and moved to Kern County. We had a challenge looking for a place to rent that we could afford with two kids. Then came the biggest challenge—the guaranteed jobs did not pan out. Reality hit hard! I had to scramble to find work, so I could afford the house and feed my family. Our families couldn't help us financially as they were already hard-pressed to support themselves. Times were hard. I finally found work at a lesser wage than I had expected. I decided to get back into roofing because I had experience in that field. I started roofing when I was 16 years old and knew I could make a decent amount of money. Most of the time, I worked from sunup to sundown seven days a week. Imagine what I felt like at the end of the day, not to mention how my wife must have felt dealing with the children, especially as one had special needs.

Take a moment here to stop reading and feel how the climate in my home must have been—the tension in the air even without words being spoken, the way we moved our bodies, the gestures, the expressions on our faces, the subtle color changes of our skin, the questions and responses, the frustration, anxiety, desperation, anticipation. It was fear at its best. What does that feel like? Did all this really take place? Yes! The answer is yes to all of the above.

When I'd come home from work, I would walk in with anticipation of what the day's events had brought my wife. What broke? Who did what to whom? What new developments were there in Daniel's behavior? Always in that behavior, there was something I couldn't fix. If I hadn't achieved enough in my day, I felt like a failure for sure. I could barely keep up with the bills. I was exhausted and breaking. The worst part was that I couldn't tell anyone, especially not my wife. I suffered in my own silence.

Have you ever walked into a room where there was a disagreement, and without any words being said, you could feel it in the air? How did you feel? I always had to be the strong one and allow my wife to vent so that she wouldn't have to suffer any more than she already did. I assume that most everyone feels these things at some point in their lives, but at what level? My wife and I were each caught up in our own stuff, our own survival, so that we couldn't see past what was going on or how we were affecting each other and everyone else around us. At 26 years old, I had no clue. I didn't know how I was affecting people. I thought I knew it all! What a cluster f---.

# Chapter 4

At three years old, Daniel was surrounded by his peers, cousins, and other children of all ages. We noticed how far behind he was, so we started looking for programs to help him develop more rapidly. At the time, unfortunately, Kern County didn't have programs to assist him.

Finally, we got results, and they were not what we had expected. Believe me, no parent wants to hear this. The answer that came was *autism*, a developmental neural disorder. We had no clue what the doctor was talking about. What the hell was autism? What did this mean? What could we do? Again, there were so many questions. We finally found a program that would accept Daniel. Unfortunately, that meant he had to take a bus as transporting him was too difficult for us. I couldn't imagine my tiny, little boy at four years old taking a bus to a program. Even today, I can't imagine what my son must've felt when he had to board the bus for the first time. I was so scared. Imagine a four-year-old having to board a bus and ride with total strangers. What was he thinking or feeling or asking? *Will I ever see my mom and dad again? Will I ever go back home?* Even if he wanted to talk, he couldn't because he no longer had verbal communication skills. What a total nightmare for us all!

At four and a half, he was reassessed and placed in a new program for autistic children. He expressed that he didn't want to go by way of body language and sounds. It was difficult to determine what was causing him to feel this way. Was it that he just wanted to stay home, or was it the people at the program or on the bus ride? We suspected it was the bus driver because Daniel never wanted to be near her. We weren't really sure why because of his lack of verbal skills. Secretly, I took time from work to follow the bus to make certain that my son was being taken care of. I had no idea with whom he was interacting while waiting for the bus, while on the bus, or while at school. I was so afraid for him.

I noticed that he was aware that others viewed him differently. He would get frustrated when he said hello and people ignored him. He would react to people who stared at him. His depth perception was also an issue, and he walked slower than most. He'd stop to look at a curb before stepping up or down move slowly as if he were feeling his way to the top or the bottom. He even approached doorways carefully. I had to pick him up at escalators because the movement was too fast for him the figure out, so I placed him on the step at the start and then took him off at the end.

So, imagine my son's world, his reality, for a moment. Here was a boy who appeared to look at the world differently from many of us. Was he more attuned to his surroundings? Had we taken things for granted? Or, was there something wrong with him? I didn't know because the doctors couldn't tell me more than the fact that he was autistic. The bottom line was that nobody knew what was really going on with him.

My suspicion, fear, impatience, and frustration came through in my actions, inactions, reactions, responses, silence, anger, envy, and jealousy. Usually, when I try to hide how I'm really thinking or feeling, I cause more confusion or conflict for others, especially for those who are counting on me

Is it possible for me to realize that there isn't anything I can do that I haven't already done? That there is nothing more important than what I'm doing at this moment? If I am stuck thinking about what I should have done, or what I think I need to do, I'm not where I need to be at this moment! Am I right or wrong? This is how I learned to be as I grew up. Do these words fit how I behaved? Or, were they just words? Without knowing it, could I be teaching an untruth? What impression would this leave on a person, like my son, who survives by his senses?

Daniel was almost five when he found a new way to change the environment by how he behaved. Some people with autism don't like to wear anything on their bodies, like jewelry, clothes, Band-Aids, and stickers. They become very upset, even frantic. Daniel was no exception. He had to be taught to wear clothes, and with any opportunity, he'd be in the buff. In his younger years, he wore shorts most of the time, and if he had a choice, he would not wear them at all. Totally uninhibited, he would walk around in the nude in the presence of anyone. It didn't matter who was there.

One day, we had company, and he stood at the end of the hallway and pulled his shorts down. Everyone reacted as he watched. Was it as shocking for him as it was for us? Did he want attention, or was he just doing what to him was natural? Was he surprised? Was he affected by the discomfort in the room? Did he sense something and remove his clothes to acknowledge it? Maybe he just wanted his shorts off.

He would stand at the curb in front of our home, watch cars go by, and drop his pants in front of the same cars every time as if he knew exactly what he was doing. Yet, I wasn't sure. It turns out that the people who were passing by were trouble in the neighborhood. Daniel continued to expose himself for a couple of years and then stopped after learning how to use his behavior as a threat. Was my son telling me something I needed to know?

What about my perception and perspective? Is it possible to accept that we can't do anything about certain behaviors and situations—that they are what they are? I didn't know the answers at the time. All I knew was that I was very protective of my son and still very perplexed with our situation. We needed help with our son and didn't know what kind or where to get it.

For birthdays and Christmases, he'd received many toys and books— things that made sounds. He would be given balls and other things that we thought he would like. We discovered that interactive things were his favorites. He would play with toys that involved other people. Toys that made noise and sounds were not of interest to him, though toys that spoke words and moved were. When we read books to him, he'd listen intently. He loved storytelling. When a conversation took place, he'd sit in and listen to the words, not necessarily watching the people speaking. When his little brother James would have playmates over, Daniel would love listening to their conversations and laughter, but he was never interested in their toys except for balls. He was pretty good at throwing a ball of any size, although he had trouble catching. We'd play make-believe pitching in the hallway. Daniel threw a hard pitch, and because he was very accurate, we'd call out strikes and balls. I was always curious and perplexed by his behaviors and interests.

I remember a conversation with my wife as Daniel was learning to throw a ball. The conversation went along the lines of why he shouldn't learn to throw with his left hand. Different things entered into the conversation like the lack of left-handed equipment. It wasn't normal. He would be less coordinated and so forth. He naturally wanted to use his left hand, yet because of the different viewpoints, I finally agreed to teach him how to throw right-handed. Secretly, I allowed him to throw with his left hand. I didn't know whether he understood the change or not, yet he learned to be accurate with both.

# Chapter 5

In October of 1984, Daniel's little sister Mary was born. Bringing her home, we saw another glimpse of Daniel's calm and love. He held her on his lap, stroked her hair, and leaned over and kissed her. He was as gentle with her as he was with James. Daniel was very loving and caring with both his siblings. As with James, I paid close attention to Daniel while he held his baby sister. I never knew if or when he'd have a fit of rage and bang his head. They were more frequent as he became older.

As the years passed, Daniel continued to have unpredictable fits and bang his head on things. I never knew what caused these events; I was more concerned about making sure he didn't hurt himself or his siblings. His rages appeared as if he were having seizures. He would come out of one and repeatedly say, "Sorry," and slap his leg when agitated. If I didn't distract him and get him involved with other things, he would go right back into another rage. All the while, we were anxious and full of apprehension. Most of the time, I would rush around as though I was holding a time bomb. The situation was exhausting, and I didn't have time to think about what was going on while it was happening. I had to take care of what was absolutely critical in the moment, and this usually involved holding him. I was his restraint when I was home, while everyone else got relief. All this took place after long, hard days of work and commuting. After everything calmed down, Daniel would go right back to being a loving and caring individual.

When Daniel was five and a half years old, his brother James was three and learning how to ride a bike. James wanted Daniel to ride, but unfortunately, we discovered that he had trouble with developing the circular motion required to peddle a bike. Later, with practice and patience, he was able to ride a three-wheeler. The three of us would ride down to the local store and buy treats for the ride back. We played tag and bump bikes; he'd laugh, and we'd all have a good time. On other occasions, he'd ride alone or with his brother. He always required prompting to go out and ride alone, as if he were anticipating something. Maybe I was projecting my fear, and he picked up on it. I really don't know what his apprehension was, only that it was there.

Daniel didn't watch a lot of television unless the Dodgers were playing. When James joined T-ball and Little League, Daniel always joined us and had a blast. He would stand behind the fence, rock from leg to leg, and fling one arm as if he were pitching or throwing a ball. This behavior went on for most of the games. He'd stand close enough to the dugout to listen to the boys talking. On occasion, he would put his hand in his mouth and try to bang his head on the fence. I assumed he was overstimulated at the game.

I made a lot of assumptions about the rages and head banging. At home, I thought he'd bang his head because he wanted something or didn't want to do something. Or, he could be anxious that someone was visiting or about to arrive. The same thing happened during conversations about where we were going next, what was coming up the next day, what happened a moment ago—and the list continued.

Most of us can verbalize these situations, but without verbal skills, he couldn't express himself any other way. At least, that's what I thought.

James began to play hockey, and of course, Daniel went along. He would say "Hi" to everyone who walked by. Some would shrink back, and others would respond to him, and when they did, he would say "Hi" repeatedly. I started coaching, and Daniel had a ringside seat. He'd sit with the players, listen to all the conversations, and then interact with them. This made him very happy, yet on occasion, he would fly into a rage or tantrum.

When he was younger, the rages lasted up to 10 minutes. As he got older, they increased in severity, and some would last for an hour and a half before subsiding. I had to hold him, so he wouldn't hurt himself or others. We experimented with headgear and other apparatuses. He'd be good for 20 minutes, a couple of hours, or half a day. Rarely did we have a day that he didn't have at least three episodes.

The doctors' only recommendation was medication to slow down his aggression, and we felt that would hinder his ability to be present. We didn't want him drugged, acting like a zombie to appease us, not to mention the potential destruction to his body. Others suggested we ignore his behavior, assuming that they were only tantrums and he would outgrow them. This was a good theory but not practical in the moment. As he got older and heavier, I started having difficulty restraining him and wondered how long this could go on.

Eventually, my wife and I gave in and put him on medication, mostly in the form of pills. He wouldn't swallow pills, so we had to crush them so he could ingest them. Initially, the medications slowed him down, but as time progressed, this was no longer the case, so experimentation with medications began. Some were successful for brief periods, except when he had a cold or any other illness, and some increased the rages. The meds would only work up to about four months. And God forbid if he needed a surgical procedure or dental work.

On one occasion, before a dental procedure in a hospital setting, we instructed the doctor not to give Daniel sedatives because they would not work. But, the doctor insisted, so they gave Daniel the meds. Afterward, the doctor came out and said, "I cannot give him any more for fear of damage to his body." He apologized profusely. Daniel stayed up the rest of the day in good spirits, unlike anyone else, who would have passed out for hours. Everyone, including the anesthesiologist, thought they knew what would work, and invariably their methods did not help.

# Chapter 6

Just before Daniel turned 18, I began to give up on my marriage and myself both mentally and emotionally. I had given up on any kind of future. I'd leave home in Bakersfield at the crack of dawn, many times in the dark, then drive for a couple of hours to work on a roof all day in the hot sun or even in the snow. Then, I'd drive back only to continue working at home, fixing toilets, holes in walls and doors, replacing tubs and light switches and anything else that had been broken during my son's rages. I felt there had to be more to life than this. Yet, I was no longer important to me. I had decided that I would never get anything I wanted, and if I did, I would not recognize it anyway. There was no point to anything. I was ready to die if that was what was to come next. I began looking outside of myself for something to make life worthwhile. I started buying things, including a boat, thinking this stuff would make me feel again, only to discover that these were just things. This was similar to when I gave my son things, and he would look at them and walk away.

Finally, I arrived home at the end of a hard day, like any other day, and Daniel told me to "Go to work" just like any other day. I told him, "No, I'm done for the day." I felt physically exhausted and conflicted, except this time, Daniel suddenly went into a rage that lasted an hour and 30 minutes. He stopped and then began to rage again. Imagine: Daniel was 25 years old, 5 feet, 11 inches tall, and he weighed 220 pounds. I weighed 225 pounds and was six feet, three inches tall. He was full of adrenaline, and I had to work really hard to keep his hands and feet from flailing and his head from banging. I stopped, looked at him, started to cry, and said, "I can't do this anymore." I lay down next to him, saying to myself that it didn't matter. In that moment, he stopped, looked at me, gave me a big hug, and said, "Sorry, Daddy." We lay there for a few minutes, and for the rest of the evening, he did not rage. There was wisdom in Daniel that I had not realized.

At 28 years old, Daniel was still raging. The experimentation still continued with the drugs, but the rages increased to up to 10 a day. I kept asking, "When is this going to stop? What are we going to do? What are we doing wrong?" The questions kept coming up because of something inside me that I still couldn't identify. The not knowing still gave me the motivation to keep trying to figure things out. I wanted to understand what was happening with my son. We all do stuff we don't understand until, one day, it became clear.

# Chapter 7

Finally, that one day came! I was at work and received a voice mail from a person who had an issue with a roof. I went over to check it out and didn't see a problem. I called back to get some clarification and set a time to meet in order to speak with the customer. I stopped by early the next morning. She let me in the door and out another door onto the deck where the problem was; she then went about her business. The job required three trips, and on the third trip, we broke into conversation about my life and my son's situation. The conversation seemed to last five minutes but was really an hour. She asked me some powerful questions, and my curiosity kept me going back for more talks. For the first time in a long time, if ever, I felt someone heard me.

Gradually, I was motivated and inspired to explore different ways of being. I opened up and expressed things I had never dreamed of telling anyone, let alone a stranger—except this person wasn't a stranger. I felt like I had known her all my life, maybe because she was open and interested in my situation. I felt like I had met her in a dream. I really believed that! I shared with her that, sometimes, I wished I could run away and that it didn't matter if I died. I was tired—tired of the life I was living. She listened and allowed me to express anything, and I even cried. I felt seen and heard for the first time in my life!

She asked me, "What would you be doing if you weren't in this life as it is?"

I told her, "I don't know."

She asked me, "What are your dreams? What do you crave? What do you see yourself doing?"

I kept responding with, "I don't know." I didn't know, nor did I have a desire to know; I didn't have any answers.

Then she said, "You can choose to do whatever you want in this life. No one can dream for you. No one can make you do anything. No one has your answers."

One of the most important things I heard her say was, "You didn't do anything wrong."

I froze for a moment. I asked her to repeat what she had just said. And she did! She said, "You didn't do anything wrong!" I broke down in tears. She went on to say, "What happened has happened to get you to this point. You don't have to do anything right now. Really, you don't. All you have to do is be with what is here, right now, in this moment. How about we start here? Will you take a deep breath?"

I listened. I did take a deep breath and discovered I was breathing in my throat. She taught me a breathing technique that has served me well since. We continued these conversations for about three months.

She asked me, "What makes you stay in your situation if it's that bad?"

I said, "Who would want someone with so much baggage?"

She then asked, "Could you leave your baggage at the door when you go home at the end of the day?"

I looked at her not really understanding what she was getting at. How could I leave the baggage at the door when the baggage was going back home?

Finally, I started to feel again as my mental state became calmer and clearer. I told her that I had already left my marriage emotionally and mentally and now wanted to physically leave.

She expressed, "Leaving is not your answer as you'll take the baggage with you wherever you go. You can change your life right where you are. This is not the time. What is your plan?"

I knew leaving was my answer, and I knew I had to try. I planned to leave in about six months. I knew I had to finish some projects to make sure my wife didn't have to struggle and to make room for a full-time caregiver. But, within a couple of months, my wife told me to leave. She knew I wasn't happy and wanted me to figure out what I wanted.

I spoke with a friend about moving into the place he was building. It was unfinished and not exactly where I would choose to live. Yet, it had running water, a bed, a shower down the hall, and a functioning kitchen. I also spoke to my friend Ann and told her what was going on. She invited me to stay at her house. I was not sure about that move, yet with uncertainty, I accepted.

I moved out of our family home, taking only clothes, paperwork and the tools of my trade. I became enmeshed in a whirlwind of emotions. I started to live again, or so I thought.

I tried many new things, even different foods, clothes, and social affairs. The commute was a lot shorter, so I had time to do more things. I slept and rested like never before. Suddenly, I had more time to think.

I noticed that I was fabricating numerous thoughts that wouldn't stop. I realized that, rather than a doer, I had had become a thinker about what I needed. These thoughts where my critic. I was becoming lost. I was becoming envious, but I was fighting it.

Like a chameleon who changes its skin color to blend in with its surroundings to hide from any creature that might want to consume it, so I became.

As I viewed the people around me, I became confused by their opinions but I assumed their thoughts, and I began to blend in. I started to hide in fear of how I might be viewed, so I had to change to blend in. I began looking to others, so I could blend in the way I chose to. Because of this, I became critical of who I was, and realized that I was allowing others to create me.

All the while, I was denying my soul because I didn't want to be seen. I've heard the phrase, "I think, therefore I am." and it was in thought that I would create who I wanted to be. But, what I didn't know was this: Who was I?

I was not like anyone else, but I chose to create myself to be like everyone else to blend in! All the while, I felt something missing. I had buried my soul in my confusion and fear. I was not real, rather all self-centered in how well I blended in. Not wanting to be alone, I allowed others to influence my thoughts for self-creation. I created the amazing chameleon and buried my soul.

Approximately three months after moving in with Ann, it was a couple of days before New Year's. She spoke these words: "I want to be taken care of. I deserve to be taken care of!" This put me in major confusion as I could hardly take care of myself. I became emotional. I could not see myself dragging her into my financial difficulties and my suffering. We were both emotional at the time, and I made a decision. She left for an engagement, and while she was gone, I loaded up my truck and moved my stuff to my buddy's house. I called my ex-wife and told her that I was coming home. While I was on the freeway, I received two calls that I did not answer; I was an emotional wreck. I answered the third call, and Ann told me she was starting to make plans for New Year's. She'd decided that she wanted to spend New Year's with me. Because I had left, this was not to be.

After New Year's Ann and I had a long talk, where she explained what taking care of her meant. I returned to Ann's place, this time leaving my stuff at my buddy's house. While at Ann's house, my divorce was finalized. I didn't know what was happening to me except that I knew I had to follow my heart. What was my heart really telling me? I couldn't recognize which was speaking to me—my heart or my monkey mind. I didn't know the difference.

Upon returning from projects to Ann's, I was met with questioning. This questioning made me feel as though I needed to hide. As I have learned to watch body language and gestures from Daniel, I felt my honest responses wouldn't be accepted. So, I became guarded, and this left Ann with assumptions. She didn't believe I was speaking the whole truth; that I was lying. This left the door open for her to think whatever she wanted to think. As I watched her, I became more and more aware of her thoughts, and my envy and jealousy where growing. I fought these feelings, but I was losing. We had given each other a commitment during the course of time, and approximately eight and a half months later, she asked for her commitment back. I was hurt deeply, and yet in that moment, I saw her as the shot sparrow gasping for breath. I knew I had to let her go. I was not good, and I was no good for her. This time, I returned to my family. I took a book that I had started reading. In the book were many affirmations to help me connect the dots to all that was unfolding and evolving in my life. The title was *A New Earth* by Eckert Tolle.

Abruptly, while working in the backyard one afternoon, I got a glimpse of what Jesus and Ann were talking about, "Love of self first, then others." Or, know my thoughts first, then that of others. I identified viscerally with that statement and could now see partially what I was missing. I was finally able to see that the thinker, the monkey mind, was causing all my problems. I was caught up in thought. My mind was not allowing me to be who I really was.

When I realized how I was thinking and what I was creating from my thinking, I immediately went inside and engaged with Daniel in a whole different way. I was fully present with him now and helped him to see where he was in his thoughts. When he would go to the past or the future, I'd bring him back by asking him where he was in that moment. That is when I knew he got it. His whole body relaxed, and he laughed as if he knew that I finally got it! He understood as I had. It was that simple. The funny thing was that I hadn't realized all the little thoughts that go on in our heads that build on each other.

Recognizing this made me come up with a key word for Daniel when I noticed him going into a stare or getting anxious. I would say, "Bullshit!" He would stop and laugh. So, all this time, Daniel had been living with all these little thoughts, and that's what would put him in a rage. The word *bullshit* brought him back to the present. He and I were now able to relate to each other!

Now, 29½ years later, I am now able to help Daniel identify other thoughts he is having. What a relief for us—and actually for everyone. Since that afternoon, we communicate on a whole different level from a place of knowing deep within. The rages began to stop and are now not as intense as they were. When he starts to go into a rage, I immediately say, "Bullshit!" That helps him identify what is bothering him. It could be as simple as feeling guilty after breaking a wall or anticipating a doctor's appointment or not going to a program the next day or something that took place the day before. Because he doesn't have clear verbal skills, I still find it difficult to pinpoint the causes. That is when I have to go deeper into the rabbit hole to understand more clearly what some of his other thoughts might be. He lives in a world full of anticipation and guilt, and I never knew to what extent until now.

Daniel has the most incredible sixth sense, an intuition beyond measure. He sees and hears much more clearly than most of us. He knows what really matters. Part of what I believe his rages are about is that he already knows what is important, and I believe we confuse him. In the past, I'm sure he was telling us, in his own way, that we were stressing and worrying more than we needed to, and that was stressing him. I believe that what was going on in his world was a reflection of how we were feeling and behaving. All he wanted was for us to be present with him in the moment. In the process, he questioned everything about himself. Did we make him feel he wasn't enough? Did he wonder why he was different from others? Who knows what he was really thinking and feeling? How many of us are holding onto the tiniest thoughts or huge thoughts and don't even know they are there? How many times do we not know how we're affecting others, let alone ourselves?

I stayed with my family for another six months and discovered that I needed to live alone so that I could continue exploring and writing this story. I couldn't blame it on Daniel, my ex-wife, the long, exhausting commute, my family, or anyone else. I also noticed subtle changes in my ex-wife. She was becoming what she thought she needed to be for me, and that was not OK. I felt trapped and confined, like I was suffocating. I found myself needing space, so I could silence my mind. I wanted to discover how I was thinking, not why I was thinking, and listen to what my thoughts were creating. The reality is that we create, good or bad, right or wrong, with our own fears and thoughts. All this thought keeps us from being whole, keeps us doing instead of being, keeps us from getting to know who we really are, keeps us from knowing ourselves, keeps us from our truth.

I once heard Ann say, "I didn't know to know," about something that happened to her in the past. I now use that statement when I realize something I didn't know and now know. She also reminded me to leave my baggage outside the door before moving into my next place. I finally got it! I was creating a situation from my thoughts without the insight that I have now.

# Chapter 8

In the earlier days dealing with my son, I had to ask myself what was more important: getting him to fit into society's ways or making him comfortable with who he is. The whole underlying tone of this book is about a search I'm putting myself through. Does everyone go through this, or do some of us already know or choose not to know about how we affect and are affected by society's ways. Do we know our impact? We are born helpless, intuitive, and uninhibited. Then, we listen with ears, watch with eyes, and learn to manipulate and survive. Then, we become aware of death, and we're uncertain about what really happens to our bodies, to our person. We've been told that we go to heaven and that dying as part of what happens to all of us. For me then, death was very real and an eventuality that was unbearable. That fact made a huge impact at a very early age.

I mentioned earlier that, when I was five or six years old, as my father drove away. I stood there and cried until I couldn't see him anymore. I was confused and frightened. I started having nightmares. I felt trapped and afraid of the unknown. I felt unprotected and wondered what was going to happen to me without my father. As I went through life, that fear dictated how I reacted to things. It was now a feeling in thought. Tolle refers to the ego as the "unconscious controlling factor." His interpretation of ego helped me to open my eyes considerably about how I allowed fear to control my every thought. I recommend Eckhart Tolle's, *A New Earth* if you want to better understand the ego and how it affects us and how we affect others.

The word *fear* resonates better than ego, so I'll be using fear from now on as I continue to write.

Recently, I sat with the tax person and listened as she told me that I owed tons of money. This was late 2009. I was in disbelief and went into reaction mode. She essentially told me that, if I didn't pay my taxes right away, something bad was going to happen to me. That automatically set me off into a place of fear—fear for myself and for my family without enough money to support them, especially for my son who might lose his home, where he was safe and secure. I allowed fear to consume me. All I have ever wanted was to take care of my family. Times were hard. Everyone was hit in the economic downturn of 2008. It was another nightmare! In this place of fear, I was swimming in a cesspool of feelings that I was not good enough, I was a failure, and I was worthless. I thought, *I'll go to jail, and who will take care of my family? I'm not smart. I'm broke.* I became consumed with fear. I lost myself for the better part of a day. Whew! What a bunch of craziness! I decided to go to bed. I slept for hours, awakened, then went right back to bed. When I finally woke up the next morning, I was in a new place. The fear was gone, and I was back to my old self. In my fear, I had become reactive in thought as to what could happen. I was making the thought real in the moment. We get so anxious and confused with jealousy, envy, possessions, aggressions, and unhappiness all because we're stuck in fear—the what-ifs of the future. Usually, we attempt to deny or escape the unknown, where most of our fears lie.

Remember the incident when I was trying to stop my son's rage. I finally said, "I can't do this anymore," and lay down next to him, saying to myself that it didn't matter. In that moment, he stopped, looked at me, gave me a big hug, and said, "Sorry, Daddy." I had rolled right out of fear into acceptance and didn't realize that it could be the beginning of a new way of being with him.

I finally realized that we were both stuck in a battle of wills, stuck with our fears. Initially, he was triggered by something he saw or what someone said and went right into fear. I was already exhausted from a hard day and didn't have much left. I was afraid and wanted to make sure that he didn't hurt himself or others. I now realize that all he wanted was for me to be real with him, to be present with him, to listen and understand. Being overprotective causes one to always want to fix things. Whew! What an amazing discovery!

What makes us think that we can fix people when people are not broken? I didn't realize I was overprotective of my son's well-being until now. Who was I really protecting? Myself, of course! I was stuck in my own fear that others wouldn't accept him, respect him, or treat him kindly. Why? Because he was different? So what that he was different! I surely didn't know how else to be. I only wanted to be the best father I could be. These were all my wants.

My son's intuitive and social skills are far greater than any of ours, even though we think we know it all. He picks up on people's expressions and body language and listens intently when others speak. He is aware of many other things that most of us don't even notice.

Recently, my son stayed the night with me. That afternoon, I had mentioned that a split-eared rabbit came up on the porch each morning. Before we went inside, the split-eared rabbit showed up on the porch, so

Daniel was able to see and watch him hop around. I then took him on a tour of the house, showed him the exposed wires on the staircase, and the location of the bathroom. I showed him where I'd be in the morning, sitting on the tailgate of my truck, drinking coffee and watching the rabbits play. He seemed good with all that, and we went to bed. I left the light on in the bathroom and in the bedroom, and he knew that I turned off the lights in the bedrooms before I left. In the morning, I sat on the tailgate of the truck and went into thought. I had a vivid thought regarding his waking up in a strange room, walking out of the bedroom, touching the exposed wires, and falling down the stairs. Suddenly, I jumped off the tailgate and started toward the house. Then, I stopped in my tracks and thought, *What the heck am I doing?* I had gone directly into my own fear and was reacting to the possible scenarios in my imagination, my thoughts. He knew me well enough to know that the lights would be off if I had left the house. So, I took a deep breath walked back to the tailgate, sat down, and wrote about that experience. This visceral experience confirmed that I had a choice to either go to fear or allow things to be as they are. My son awakened with a big, fat smile on his face. We went to have breakfast and had a fantastic day. If I had not realized that I had gone to fear, I would've screwed up the whole day!

I also remember when Daniel held his baby brother and sister—the loving looks, hair strokes, and the kisses on their sweet faces—all the while watching in anticipation that he might hurt them. He would be in a very calm loving and peaceful place, holding his siblings, while I was stuck in fear. The longer he held them, the more I would grow anxious. Eventually, I would take the babies from him for their safety. Or, was it for my own security? In those moments, did I create fear in him? Did I make him feel not good enough? Did I hold him back from being who he really was, a boy who was not inhibited but was expressive in every way? Those precious moments were lost in fear. My wife and I were always left with sadness, guilt, and questions: Are we doing this right? What are we doing wrong?

What I've come to realize is that, when I'm stuck in fear, it includes jealousy, envy, rejection, and expectation. I'm not seeing others as they really are. I know can't control how others interpret my actions, and I'm not responsible for how others react or respond. And, what I do know for sure is that my impact is important. What I say is critical! Do I want to present myself full of fear or good with myself?

# Chapter 9

There was peer pressure where I lost myself to others. I was too fat or too skinny, had crooked or missing teeth, wore glasses, had the wrong clothes or hair, and the list of defects went on. I got so hung up on what others thought of me that I lost sight of what was really important. I was afraid of being judged by others, so I made choices allowing others to dictate how I should look and act. I held myself back with fear. Did I really like the trends at that time? Or, was I following the trends because everyone else was? What kept me from being me? My own thoughts based in fear prevented me from being authentic and genuine.

Let's play with the word *judge* and see where it takes us. There is the usual negative judgment that makes us defensive, and there is positive judgment, which can also trigger defensiveness. It all depends on whether or not someone listens and hears what the other person is really saying or if he or she is stuck in some want. Some people aren't used to being complimented and react; negative judgment comes from a place of fear.

Stop for a moment, and take a look around you. It's OK. No one knows what you're doing.

Now, notice what's going on around you. Don't judge yet; only notice. What's going on from where you're sitting in your perspective? What colors do you notice? What do you see and hear? Now, judge what you see. Is it positive or negative or both? We are making judgments all the time whether we know it or not. Just the negative or positive is a judgment.

As mentioned earlier, Daniel is a big guy. He loves to laugh and sing. He can sometimes be loud when expressing himself, not realizing his impact. He loves to interact with people. He is compassionate and sensitive to people's feelings. We have gone to stores or other public places, and people stare at him or withdraw or are curious or genuinely say hello. He lets me know when he's uncomfortable or upset by hiding his head under his T-shirt or displaying some other body language or gestures.

Some people have stopped us and asked what is wrong with him: What does he have, or what is his diagnosis? Depending on how the question is asked, I either get defensive or openly share that he is labeled autistic. Some people respond with, "What a gift." I have asked myself, *What do they see?* Do they realize what a challenge it is to have a child with autism in this society, with its frustrations, doctors, behaviors, and mental stresses? The reality is that autistic children don't fit into society's way of thinking.

I sometimes question how my son's life will progress based on my experiences with society and my teachings from childhood to adulthood. Children are born with a natural curiosity. As some children begin to develop, their parents and other people influence them, dictate how they'll behave. Usually, by the time they become adults, their natural ability to be curious has become lost.

Imagine this for a moment: I'm working extremely hard to provide for my family, barely making ends meet. The children are now in school, listening to their peers talk about all the stuff they have or don't have. My top priority as an adult male is to provide for my family no matter what their needs are—new clothes, games, toys, food, and shelter to name a few.

I learned to manipulate and play the game to stay ahead. How many of us have played keeping up with the Joneses? As a parent, I wanted the best for my children. I wanted them to have all of the things the other children had. Without knowing it, I was teaching them how to do the same thing to their own children. Some parents want their children to follow in their footsteps. I did not want my children to go into my line of work. I wanted them to go to college and not have to labor so hard for living. My son James decided to go into roofing, even though I preferred he didn't. I knew he could use his talents for something better and easier. But, I also knew that he needed to do his own thing and be his own person. Children want to please their parents and, for the most part, can lose themselves and forget who they are or who they want to be. They become confused about what they know is important to them, and they forget their curiosity and perfect self-expression.

The need to get approval from an outside source starts very early in childhood then moves right into adulthood. I allowed people's words to affect how I felt about myself. Like a subtle brainwashing, not realizing it was taking place, I allowed people to manipulate my thoughts and talk down to me. They made me think they were better than me through their words, possessions, and social groups. I allowed myself to be manipulated because of many different fears, such as rejection or abandonment.

In my opinion, children already know what's *good* or *bad* and *right* or *wrong*. I have used these labels to express a point. There is no good or bad or right or wrong! These are judgments! A lot of us do not know about instinct and intuition or feeling, though we all have them. You know that feeling you get in your gut that's telling you something isn't safe, or not to go forward with something, and you do anyway. We are born with instincts and intuition and naturally know the difference between what is safe and what is not. Unfortunately, we are taught very early in childhood to go against ourselves by stepping into fear and guilt, shame and embarrassment, asking why or what our friends would do. What makes use teach our children those destructive lessons?

I have come back to that place of knowing to know. I learned about fear and guilt through my parents very early in my childhood and then projected them onto my children. I became protective, even overprotective, of my children's well-being and welfare. I became a thinker regarding fear during my childhood then taught my children to think and fear. In my judgment, the confusion as to what to be or what to do to please my parents became my focus, and I lost sight of what really mattered to me. Then, I started feeling like something was missing. I didn't know where to look, so I started looking outside of myself for answers. I continued thinking instead of being with what was in the moment. I didn't have to look outside for answers. The answers were always inside of me. The answers are in each of us individually!

I was born naturally creative, as we all are. I knew what I liked and what I didn't like. I knew what my interests were very early in my life, and then I got consumed with what others were doing or saying. Really, all I wanted was to be all that I am and to be allowed to feel what I felt. All of us want that.

Society and religion attempt to put us in little boxes called *normal*. What is normal anyway? So, what about you do wish to be normal? My son has not been referred to as normal. He has been labeled autistic, which in some circles is considered abnormal. Fortunately, he is not normal as I wouldn't want to take away his natural ability to be. All he wants is to be seen and heard for who he is, to know that I care about him. He doesn't care what I'm thinking, but he does know what I'm feeling, and that is what's important to him.

Let's assume for a moment that we are all born "normal," that that is right and good, and everything else is irrelevant. Who sets the standard for normal? One person's opinion or some majority? Some say animals don't think, yet they travel in flocks, schools, and herds not unlike people, who choose to be with others like them. The animals tend to stay in their own groups, mate and play with their own kind, and guard their young from others that don't appear to be of the same kind. Some animals will kill their young because they appear different, sick, or weak. How they are perceived is not unlike what we do to humans with "handicaps." We determine who is "normal" by the way one thinks and behaves, and we label people by their functioning levels of intelligence and appearance in comparison to everyone else.

Next time, notice when someone is speaking. Is there a subtle shift in his or her eyes, hand gestures, and other body movements? Are there voice tone shifts that do not match what they're saying? There's a difference that tells you the speaker is not really present with you—maybe physically present, and that's about it. What about that person isn't convincing? It's like watching a bad actor playing a part in a movie or a play. That's not who the person really is. He is only an actor. In a conversation, those same feelings come into play. When we're sensing the environment, we can assess what's going on all around us. A blind person listens for tones in voices and knows where those voices are coming from. He can sense what is going on around him. A person without verbal skills does the same thing. Daniel focuses on eye contact and body language and also senses body energy. Both of them can tell whether you're really in the present with them or whether you're preoccupied with something else.

Fortunately, Daniel was stubborn and didn't let his feelings go unnoticed, whether through rages, tantrums, or silence. He wasn't willing to compromise or sacrifice his intuition for the sake of making us happy or seeking our approval. Yet, part of him was uncertain and confused because the majority of people said there was something "wrong with him." Even we were uncertain. And that is where his critical saboteur worked against him; guilt and self-doubt surfaced.

When we are children, our parents are our guardians. They tell us what we should and shouldn't be doing—don't do this; don't do that. We observe them and notice that they are not practicing what they preach. Usually, a child knows if a parent is listening or not and will walk away not realizing that is the first glimpse the critic, the saboteur voice, which sometimes stays with us throughout our lives. It may then show up in an instant when we are judged positively or negatively. The voices in our heads start telling us, *You don't matter. That person she's talking to is more important than you. You're not worthy. You are wrong. You are bad.* Some of us keep this in our pockets throughout adulthood. The truth is that we do matter, we are important, we are worthy and deserving of consideration, and there is no right or wrong, good or bad." This is all made-up stuff. I had to go deeper into the rabbit hole to unlearn what I was taught as a child, so I could realize what my fears had created.

So, when do you become defensive? Who are your critics and saboteurs? What are they telling you? Notice what happens to you when someone is speaking to you. Are they speaking with you? Are you noticing their sensations or feelings? Is anything coming up for you? Are you reacting, becoming defensive, or preparing to respond before the person is finished with what he or she is saying? Notice and see what happens.

I spent many years watching Daniel, his body movements, and the things he did and didn't do. There was something very real that I failed to notice due to his lack of verbal skills. As Ann entered the picture, she was very expressive. Do you recall when I came back from working on projects, and I said I was being questioned? As the questions were being asked, I noticed the subtle shifts in her body gestures and movements. This was where I knew I had to watch what I said for fear of how she might take it. Her subtle shifts were also the catalyst for the first connection with Daniel because those shifts were very similar to Daniel's.

I was beginning to hear without ears, see without eyes, and was sinking deeper into the rabbit hole.

# Chapter 10

Each of us is born uniquely different. There are so many words to describe what we feel when we touch something, and most of us will not see the same thing in the same way. Let's take some of the studies out there that have shown that, when five people watched an accident occur, each one expressed something different. Some of these studies show that people see different colors on the same people. Everyone involved in the study has his or her own perspective based on where he or she was during accident, and each has a different perception or assumption based on how he or she was feeling or what he or she was thinking at the time. So, who then decides who is correct? Because each saw something different, what does that tell us about what is normal" and who might be considered handicapped?

By labeling, we categorize people based on their capacities or levels of learning, forgetting that each person has his or her own perspectives, perceptions, and assumptions based on how he or she was born, raised, and treated.

The moment a child behaves differently from the majority, it is usual to automatically assume that something is "wrong" or that he or she is handicapped and not "normal." Some of us depend on medical professionals to give us answers, believing they know what is normal based on their education and training. We take our children to doctors, specialists, and other medical professionals in an attempt understand the problem, not noticing or checking in with the child. What about the child's feelings, perceptions, and assumptions about what is taking place? What about the child who may not be expressing fear, confusion, or conflict? What are we imprinting or insinuating about the child? What about the guilt the child may be feeling as he believes he did something wrong or created this problem? Are all these questions being the verified by the parents' behavior, including ignoring the child while having conversations as if the child were not present? Whether a child likes it or not, he or she is there for the ride.

What if the child doesn't believe there is anything wrong yet is influenced by others? We allow other's opinions to dictate how we feel, what we see, and how we hear, and thus, we often lose confidence in ourselves.

What is wrong here? Who said we aren't good enough? Was it someone next door, a mother, a father, a sibling, friend, relative, a teacher, a preacher, or the ice cream man who made a lasting impression on us? What about the fear instilled in us by our own thinking? The choice I made in not wanting to be alone, when I allowed myself to fit into the majority's way of thinking, became that little voice in my head that somehow took control of my life, my way of being. Somehow, I was not OK because I wasn't this way or that way. I didn't do it the way everyone else did. Fortunately, I have awakened from this voice of fear.

You know the old saying, "If it's not broken, don't fix it." Well, I spent most of my life trying to fix things that weren't broken, including my son's situation. Early on in my roofing career, I'd see what appeared to be a potential leak or problem, and I'd fix it immediately, or so I thought. Invariably, the repair would cause more problems down the road. One day, I finally realized I was creating more problems, so now, I leave things alone when it appears to be only a potential problem. So, what prevented me from that wisdom early on in my son's situation?

Earlier, I mentioned the time when Daniel was learning to throw a ball. He would naturally use his left hand, and he was good at it. We decided to make him use his right hand whether he understood the reasoning or not. Was this evidence that we were trying to fix what was not broken? Did this need to change the way he did things have a negative influence?

When people appear to be abnormal or dysfunctional physically, mentally, or emotionally, or appears to be handicapped, are they broken? Do they need to be fixed? On many occasions, I have noticed that people react to my son, even step back or to the side to avoid him, and I've heard comments like, "He is weird. He looks strange. He's not all there. He's a dummy," as if he were different from them, contagious, or from another planet. When my son would say "Hi" to people, the majority would ignore him and walk away. I don't know about you, but I sure wouldn't feel good about myself if I were in those people's shoes. Both my son and I were affected by such cruelty. Of course, a person has the right to respond or not, and what does that say about the majority of our society? Over the years, I've watched many interviews with disabled individuals who improved their situations. They were tearful and said that all they ever wanted was to be heard and seen as normal human beings. Most said, "No one would listen to me. No one would talk to me. I was treated like a freak, and I just wanted to be loved." These disabled, handicapped, autistic, disfigured, or otherwise different people have been labeled, but they have feelings and emotions just like the rest of the human race. They are no different than the rest of us who have not been labeled. What makes our perceptions of someone else right or wrong? Again, we are born not thinking. We learn from our experiences, fear, and wanting what is "right or wrong," and as we continue to grow, we learn from all those critics around us. Next time, notice how you feel when you see or are confronted by a handicapped person. What is your initial response or reaction? What do you see or hear? What is your reaction based on—your intuition, feelings, or your fear?

As I continue to sit and evaluate how I think about things and what my thoughts create, I ask, *How much of what I experience is real or an illusion self-created in thought and fear?* Do I feel anxious? Is there something that I need to be doing right now? And, what is creating this? What is wrong with right now?

# Chapter 11

It was the day before New Year's Eve (2010), and time was ticking away. I was still asking that damn question, *How deep does the rabbit hole go?* Ann invited me to dinner to express her appreciation and gratitude. As she prepared dinner, we talked, and the phone rang. She answered, and her excitement rose as she spoke about the luncheon she was attending the next day. I heard her say she wasn't sure what she'd wear, but it "had to be nice and sexy." Clearly, she wanted to impress someone, and it was not I! I knew who it was. She had celebrated New Year's Eve with this person two years prior. But, she'd invited me to dinner tonight. I noticed a shift in her demeanor, or was it mine? I was in conflict about the whole thing. I held back from asking her out on New Year's Eve. As we shared the meal, so many thoughts went through my head. Rather than making assumptions, I chose to enjoy the time we had together, even though it was brief and emotionally and mentally difficult for me. Clearly, she had other plans for New Year's Eve because she'd invited me for this evening instead. As much as I wanted to invite her out for New Year's, I knew not to, as something in me said, "No!"

I didn't know whether it was my saboteur telling me I wasn't good enough, fear of being rejected, or just a gut feeling. I left there in conflict, confused about what I was doing there. Did I make all this up? Where did I go while my body was sitting there? Certainly, I was in deep thought somewhere else. I was projecting assumptions and perceptions about her, or did I want something else? My thoughts and feelings ran rampant then stopped as if I had hit another wall of the rabbit hole. It was clear we are not a couple, so I had to let her live her life without me.

There I sat on my first New Year's Eve alone with my thoughts. So, I put in a movie to drown out the thoughts. Never in the past had I ever thought about spending this night alone. I always had my family, and there were never any questions as to whether I'd sleep through New Year's or not. I felt I had to spend the night alone, not knowing why. There was still something missing in my life, and I couldn't put my finger on it, though I felt I was onto something. Initially, I felt calm and relaxed. Then, different thoughts and questions fled through my mind, such as, *Where can I go? What can I do? Shouldn't I be spending this so-called special night with friends and family?*

I answered the questions rationally and changed my perspective on how I thought about where I was, releasing the want. I found resolve and then relaxed again. I received a phone call with an invitation to celebrate the New Year with champagne and family. Immediately, I said, "No thank you —I need to be alone," and continued watching a movie. The movie finally ended, and I turned everything off and fell asleep peacefully.

Suddenly, I wakened at 4:30 a.m., flat on my back, raging and yelling, "Knock it off!" As I sat up and looked at the pillow, I stopped and asked, "What the f--- just happened?" I felt mentally and emotionally divided as if two parts of me where in a battle or wanted to merge. In my gut, I felt two separate beings. What the hell just happened? At whom was I yelling? No one else was there, yet I swore there was someone else present. I sat there quietly allowing myself to breathe and feel all that had happened during that morning. Was I dreaming or imagining all that stuff? Was any of it real? I came to realize that I had awakened in a battle between feelings, which I am, and thoughts, which I am not! These two parts are what kept me stuck in confusion about who I was and how I knew myself and others. In that moment of awakening, that monkey mind kept feeding me thoughts like a freight train out of control. The issues that arose that morning came from a deeper place of knowing. Literally, there was a divide between knowing and reasoning. That kept me from loving.

I wanted so much to be with Ann and to share the deep caring I felt for her. In that desire, I was self-centered. It was my desire, my want in thought. In my thoughts, I began to judge. In my fear, I didn't want to be alone.

The scared, envious monkey mind, or the little voice, was feeding me information about what others might be thinking of me. It was attempting to lead me astray from what I knew. I knew Ann would not intentionally harm me. I was now seeing the thoughts that kept feeding me information that I might be betrayed by Ann. Ann was not mine, and in my want, I was possessive in what I wanted. If she cared about me, how could she do this? That was thought, not me! In doing this, was she even a friend? Again, thought, not me! In going after what she wanted, how was I being portrayed? Thought, not me! Was she lying about how she felt about me? Thought, not me!

The monkey mind's freight train ran into a wall, "Knock it off!" Due to her actions, I was now seeing the illusion created by me alone! I was not allowing! I was in my own want. In want, I judged in fear of not wanting to be alone. It was no different than wanting my son to be OK. In my wanting him to be OK, he was not in my mind! And that led him to be confused or to think he was not OK in comparison to everyone else. I couldn't see that he was OK. His body wasn't working as everyone else's, yet he was all there!

Prior to this New Year's, I had made many changes in my life. I had stepped into the fear of being alone. I had left the family. I moved so that I could be by myself and follow what was happening to me. I had confronted the fear alone. While in this new place, I was amazed by the many bats flying around, while I was outside. The fear I had of them made me go inside because they were flying within a foot or so of me. One evening, I went outside, not caring what they might do to me. I forgot my fear, and amazingly, the bats were nowhere around! They were attracted to the fear. I had also not realized I was like my son, alone in my thoughts. I was also still helping Ann with some of her projects. She was very expressive and open with her feelings and thoughts as we worked together. I saw her innocence. I enjoyed the time we shared without negative thoughts. Yet, there was a part of me that still wanted something. There was a missing piece that I couldn't put my finger on.

Fortunately, the painful experience on New Year's Day was the payoff for the services I provided. To my amazement, this was a huge, eye-opening experience for me. I was exhausted and could barely get myself going on New Year's Day. I sat for three days unraveling all the different illusions I had created for myself and realized how they affected every part of my life. I had already discovered the thinker before this experience, when I had helped my son see what he was creating for himself. But, until this day, I hadn't fully realized the depth of the impact.

Ann called and wished me a happy New Year, and I told her of my experience. She acknowledged my strength and courage for being with all the pain my thoughts had caused. She even said she was delighted with my progress. She asked, "What is the gift in this experience?" It was now welcomed. In the past, she'd ask me that question after I had shared a painful experience, and I'd think it was a crazy question, though I knew it had some value. Now, I see the value in all experiences, painful or not, especially from the New Year's awakening, where I viscerally experienced my "mind!" I am now able to recognize my many thoughts and how I allowed my thoughts to create my experiences. I now know that a thought is not real until I act.

When a child comes into this world not reacting or responding as others do or the way we think they should, the tendency is to think something is wrong. I didn't know my thoughts back then were that my son was broken and that I could fix him. Those thoughts were based on my own wants and the thoughts of others. I stopped seeing my son for his individuality and his brave and courageous self-expression. I was always looking at the external physical form of how he was behaving because his body didn't function like that of other children. I failed to see that there was a person, a being, inside that body who was fully functional, who understood and felt everything around him even more than I did.

Just because his body didn't function like other children's didn't mean he wasn't there. It was the contrary! His limited speech enabled other senses to become stronger, thus making his awareness extremely keen. Until now, I was incapable of seeing that the head banging and violent outbursts were misconstrued as tantrums or seizures. It was my son's way of telling me something significant. He was trying to get my attention and was letting me know that I didn't understand what was important at the time. He was letting me know that I was confusing him when I was in thought. He had the ability to feel things on a deeper level, and I was missing it. I wasn't present with him in the moment. I was preoccupied with making money to support my family, with work I had to do, and with other issues that were confronting me. I see that now. I wasn't allowing him! I wasn't allowing Ann! I was self-centered in want—my want, my fear, and my critic all were in judgment. That was not love! I've always known I wasn't here to harm anyone, but I didn't know how I was harming others and myself. I was there to care for someone. I didn't know then that I was going through a rebirth in thought. I was being shown another way—how to know real love and to see through my self-creation!

At this point, I am drawn to the story of story of Adam and Eve before they ate from the tree of knowledge. They walked around naked without a care in the world, like Daniel, and didn't need or want for anything. They were in the world with the Creator and didn't think. They were asked by the Creator not to eat from the tree of knowledge. As the story goes, Eve took from the tree and gave it to Adam, and they both ate. After eating from the forbidden tree, they felt guilt and shame and hid from the Creator, not knowing that He already knew what they had done. They had already condemned themselves—right, wrong, good, bad, blame, shame, want, don't want, fear, don't fear.

Daniel is like the original Adam and Eve, naked and free without a care in the world. He can strip down and not care or worry about what anyone else thinks. We could be standing in the middle of Times Square on New Year's Eve, and he'd strip down and not care. Daniel wears clothes because we told him he had to.

# Chapter 12

After this awakening, I found myself sitting in the morning for three hours at a time silencing my mind and asking what was next?

I was doing without want or self. Ann's projects took time. Some were more difficult than others, and I was now doing them without strings. To some, this appeared needy, to others caring, and to others, I was a fool. To me, I was in need. I needed to see through my thoughts of self. I had even moved Ann to another state and wanted nothing in return, only to find my soul. After doing these things, I would return and write about that little voice in my head and the parts I now knew as not me. I was now on a slide going deeper into the rabbit hole and enjoying the ride. Now, with both feet out of the box, the deeper I went, the more I saw myself, my son, and Ann. I was now a glutton for punishment. I now needed to see the suffering created by my thoughts.

I had experienced a divide. I thought myself to be one, when I was really two. It sounds strange—maybe I lost my mind. Had I? I was now seeing things in the only book that I had read from cover to cover almost four times. Then, I threw it aside and gave up, saying I would never read it again. Fortunately Martha, before I left the family, gave me a new Bible, which I now use as affirmation. In this new awareness, I called Ann again to ask, "Why me?"

Her response was, "Why not you?"

I was now learning to control my mind instead of allowing my mind to control me. I found that I'd been on autopilot. This happened in childhood in my first thought, which was *alone!* Not knowing who I was, I didn't want to be alone. In fear of being alone, my mind determined through everyone else what I needed to be to fit in. This was when I left my being, essence, energy, and soul behind. I became smarter in terms of how to get what I wanted. When I didn't get what I wanted, I became frustrated and angry and confused. How could I get what I wanted? I was like a child in a sandbox fighting over a toy. No wonder the Bible referred to me as a child even though I liked to think that I had grown up. In this new awareness, I realized I was given a body. Part of that body is the mind, and they are one. It's not unlike Buddhism and other beliefs in which one must release the soul or being from the mind. The object is to realize, *I am not my body.* I must be aware of what I allow my mind to create. I had allowed my mind to react out of defense, and it was guarding "innocents." But now, I am feeling Daniel's thoughts.

Now, my relationship with Daniel is great, and I have found as I talk to many people that this is not limited to Daniel or myself. This book sat in editing for a year as I continued to unbury more awareness, and in late 2011, I made the connection to *alone.*

I started a graph (see Chapter 24) that I believe now is complete. I believe it can help one realize where he or she might be. My peace now comes from within. I would love it if others could experience this peace. I would never have imagined doing something like this in my life, as I don't like to read, let alone write. Seeing people realize these a-ha moments gives me great joy. Writing this was very humbling. Life wasn't supposed to be so difficult, yet I allowed my thoughts to create difficulty.

# Chapter 13: Alone

## "To think one is alone is to be alone."

As children, we come into this world a clean slate, eyes wide open and curious, full of feeling and wonderment. Too soon, a thought creeps into our awareness. We notice that we see things differently and feel things differently from others. We begin to think that we are alone and do not fit into the world we see around us. This thought of being alone is where the shift begins. It is our first connection with self-critique, self-doubt, and the thought of different. We may also begin to feel that everyone is better than us, and everything is our fault.

It is then that we become unacceptable in our thoughts. It is in this thought of alone that we leave the feeling of togetherness and start creating separateness. We start looking to our parents for guidance; they become our role models.

This is where we leave our first love, our being.

This is why I was able to show Daniel his thought-created self-critic, his self-doubt, and his thought of being different.

This is where I came back to my being when I saw him. This is where we both returned to our being. This is where the paradoxes began and where my journey began down the rabbit hole.

What I was unaware of in childhood was that my parents were doing the best they knew how, and for the most part, they were trying to survive. I thought they knew more because of their experiences and opinions, yet most of their opinions came from their parents, who were also trying to survive. As a child, I didn't know that the subtle shift had begun. I allowed my mind to create who I thought I needed to be based on other's opinions. This was where I first allowed my mind's imagination to take control and to create something from nothing, that which I thought I needed to be. I allowed my mind to set the program for my life—surviving. This was a choice I was unaware of, and I started wanting to be like Mom or Dad or both. I started wanting approval, not realizing that I was unacceptable in my own eyes. Everyone else knew better. This was my first connection with envy and jealousy. Everyone else was better. In this place, I felt I didn't want to be who I was within my being or soul.

Think of Jesus's words, "Want not!" And my soul wants nothing; it allows. My mind shows up as my protector to survive, and the chaos begins. My mind is part of the equipment, the creator of my illusion to survive.

In judgment of myself (the self-critic), I go to fear in the realization that I am not the same as others. I begin to hide from the innocence that I have to survive. Jesus's words—judge not, fear not, want not—these words were spoken to guide me and to show me. This is how I left my being, my soul, to the equipment, my mind. I will continue in this cycle until I realize my mistake. Relationships are in the same cycle, and I kept teaching this same cycle as long as I stayed in it myself. This is why history repeats itself, this is how I kept reliving my childhood, and this is how I kept repeating the same mistakes. I want to know what makes someone else do what they do, and I don't want to know what makes me do what I do. I would rather try to get to know someone, and I thought I already knew myself. I didn't take the time to look at myself and see how I created with my choices. When I change constantly, like a chameleon, there is no peace, only chaos. In reconnecting with my soul, I find peace. There is a change needed— allowing" Now, I use the mind instead of the mind using me.

The graph I've made (see Chapter 24) is a visual to help me realize what part I have gone to, allowing me to step out of that part when I realize it.

To know we are energy, that is allowing without thought. I have allowed my mind to create alone in thought. The cycle is judgment, fear, want, and the child. If I am in one, I am in all. Here is the paradox. If I am in want, I don't want. If I am in fear, I don't want to be afraid. I am hiding in the assumed judgments of others, and I don't want others to know I am afraid. In this situation, I am oppressive to others and myself. There is no peace. To be in compassion is to step out of the fear and share with my children to help them break the cycle.

I need to tell them this: You didn't do anything wrong. It was an experience or mistake you needed so you could be where you are now.

Being in this connection with Daniel has kept me searching deeper within my self-creation. Thought can be the breakdown of my energy or the essence of who I am. To break down the false creation of self is to return to the energy that I am. To break down the thought image of self-creation is in a reference used in the Bible. "And the dead shall rise." Or, we left our souls to the tree of knowledge, which is thought.

I was dead in not knowing who I am. In regards to wanting, it has been said, "Want not." What I don't want is actually who I am! Who I am wants nothing. Because I want in the world, I want to be seen, recognized, and approved. In this attempt, I connect with the self-critic, or judgment, in viewing my environment. I must tell myself that it's OK to be me. Yet, who am I?

In the view of myself as not the same as others, I hide in the judgment of myself in fear. It comes from this feeling that I connect to thought and I create alone. This is self-centered or mind-created illusion—the thoughts of alone, want, fear, judgment, criticism, confusion, doubt, frustration, anger, envy are the mind-created self or negative energy. The references in the Bible are all truths to who we are. Knowing this helps me remember who I am— my purpose, essence, chi, energy, soul—without thought. When we let ours- elves feel deeply, beyond the self-critic, we feel our true, natural state. We feel an allowing. Out of this allowing comes peace and joy, all which is love. There is nothing to defend' no negative or protective thoughts are needed. When I'm protecting a thought that is not true, which is usually a negative thought of myself, I remember the truths of who I am. My true essence, my soul, needs no defense. In other words, break down your own self-created defenses.

By believing we're alone, in this thought, alone is created in confusion and judgment. In this alone perspective, I can't leave others alone in my fear of being alone. Noticing that I see things differently than others and seem to feel things differently than others, I think of being alone. In this feeling, I connect with the thought of alone. It's not real, yet I make it real in my wanting not to be alone. In my wanting to create togetherness, I connect with others' thoughts and opinions, attempting to be seen as OK, The paradox here is that this is where I left my essence. I connect with the judgment of myself in comparison to others in my fear of being seen as different in others' opinions. I allow others opinions to create who I think I need to be and what I need to do to be a part of a family. I then create togetherness in shared thoughts and opinions. I have now made others more important and have created a thought image of myself.

This is not real; it is only an illusion created in thought to survive. Who I was before the first thought was allowing. And, to be allowing in others' opinions is not OK. Yet, true love is allowing. No want, no fear, no judgment or self-critique—this because of the view of myself. In comparison to others, everyone was better than I was, everything was my fault, and I was wrong. This started when I wanted my parents' attention, and it was a competition with my siblings. Yet, I was unaware of it at the time. I became smarter in how to get what I wanted. I connected with money, marriage, racism, religion, and governmental beliefs, all for a sense of identity. In this process, I left my essence behind. I think peer pressure, fashion, the Joneses, opinions in church, opinions in government, even relationships are attempts to be for someone else, all in the fear of being alone. I created the illusion in my thoughts of desires. I wanted to possess that which was not mine; no one is ours to possess. In fear, I do not want to lose that which is not mine to possess. In judgment, I connected with confusion and how to get what I wanted, all from wanting not to be alone. Here again is the paradox: The soul that I am has no want, has no fear, has no judgment—these are thoughts that are not real. I allowed the mind to create for my survival. Who I am is not my mind. And a thought is not real until I act, making my want, my fear, and my judgment real. Knowing this, I have a choice, and I will not be self-centered in it. I am acting from being alone! I must choose allowing without judgment, fear, or want and to be selfless.

The flipside to allowing is what a person wants or needs from me. To simply allow or be selfless is not OK in others' opinions; in their opinion, I want something or need something from them. Now, in their fear or judgment, if I don't want anything, I must be lying.

# Chapter 14:
# Allowing

## "Allowing is who I am. What I have allowed is not who I am."

In this paradox, I have allowed the opinions of others to be my opinions. I have allowed the fears of others to be my fears. I have allowed the wants of others to be my wants. I have allowed the judgment of others to be my judge—all in my mind. This took me subtly away from who I truly am. In wanting to fit in and in not wanting to be alone, I allowed my mind to create a false me, in order to survive. In doing so, I have not allowed others to be themselves either. In allowing, there is no fear, no want, no judgment, and no thought to defend.

The thought of being alone, experienced in childhood, is where my mind began to take control and protect my soul. Though it was easier to allow my mind to take control, I didn't realize I was denying my soul.

Our souls cannot experience life if we are in survival mode. To experience is to allow breaking the cycle of want, fear, or judgment, and to break the cycle of those thoughts. We must break free of that incredible tool of the mind, which has been stuck in survival mode, and control the mind in allowing. Our souls need no defense, and the mind has been defending against others' defenses. During the proses of writing this piece, I gathered with three people. In this conversation, a heckler showed up and said, "This is different than what you have been saying." This person felt an untruth, and I found myself defending a thought put into words; that thought was not true. My mind was defending as it didn't want to be discovered. My mind was in full defense and in fear. I was trying to convince everyone of its truth. This did not feel good, yet it seemed I could not stop. The conversation stopped, as it appeared they were convinced, yet it left them questioning the truth and my credibility. I was defending and creating a story or lie, and I was no longer allowing. This is how my mind comes to my defense. Everyone and everything has a purpose' to evolve is only to allow everything and everyone their purpose. We all have different purposes. This is love—allowing. The energy that we all are is the soul. This is what we are all looking for, and in this, we are the same. The soul is allowing. This energy is you. We must take control of the mind and live to let live.

# Chapter 15: Confusion

## "In confusion, we find understanding."

Not knowing who we are and in this discovery of being alone, we begin to connect with others in their confusion in an attempt to describe ourselves. In that state, everyone around us is on a pedestal or is an authority but only because we don't know who we are. We begin creating who we think we need to be, and the mind is now in control. The essence of who we are is left behind. It connects with opinions, comments, judgments, self-criticism, fear, want, right, wrong, good, bad, assumptions, and doubts. Even OK is a judgment in comparison to what and who we are. Just to be is not OK as everyone says you have to be or do something. Again, this is possessed in someone else's opinion. In the words of a great teacher, "Judge not, lest ye be judged." In confusion, in this cycle, we allow others to feed on our fears, our wants, our criticisms, and it's the minority who are profiting from not speaking the truth. Even schools thrive in comparison, using grades to compare students. In an attempt to make us the same, churches thrive on our fear and our confusion. God and Jesus said, "Low man is become as one of us." Tough nut to swallow? Then, I guess God and Jesus lied! Yet, knowing this would stop the confusion, wouldn't it? Maybe Creator would fit better. Who's suffering, who's our own worst enemy, and who doesn't want us to know? It's better if we stay confused, isn't it? To evolve, we must let go of survival mode and live. Break free of Satan. Live and let live. Could it be as simple as knowing our own thoughts and not attempting to possess that which is not ours to possess? The battle is within. It's our own self-creation when we say we don't even like ourselves. Who's confused? In this, we are now beginning to create "human!" The loving, compassionate, humble, child or soul that I was and that we all know is now beginning to disappear into thought. God never left us; we left God!

# Chapter 16:
# Want or Desire

## "In wanting and desiring, what is, is not OK."

There are many forms of wanting, or not wanting, and in wanting, there is a desired outcome. In this desire, I began to reason. I started watching those around me and began to see how they got what they wanted. I began listening to the thoughts and opinions of others, so I could learn how to get what I wanted. What I didn't see is that there is often a deep-seated feeling of alone. In not wanting to be alone, I began to reason. I didn't want to be alone. I wanted to be approved of, so I began to feed into the thoughts and opinions of others. I created the person I thought I needed to be, so I was not alone—the creation of self! Did this result in the denial of my very soul? Yes.

This is the piece that connected me with confusion—the wanting to fit in, thinking it was not OK to be me. The desire to be more, or saying that I was not good enough, was where I began to cover up who I was. Through this wanting, I had a desired outcome to be more. Just being was not enough, especially in seeing what was happening around me. I began to mold myself into what would make others see me as OK. This was the beginning of death to my soul. It was the wanting or desiring spirit that led me into my mind or thought. In this wanting, the confusion led me to frustration, anger, jealousy, envy, the need for more, bigotry, religion, money, and possessions, so all others could see me as OK. In fearing and judgment, I myself thought, *I'm not OK.* In breaking down these truths, I came back to what was meant to be—my soul, a place where very few people go because they don't want to be alone. In finally realizing these truths, I freed myself from the constant stream of thought and now see clearly what we're all doing to each other. If we choose, there is another way. We must connect with that loving, compassionate soul that desires nothing. It allows. In this world, it means being the fool. We are alone if we say nothing. The relationships we are in are but a micro glimpse of not wanting to be alone, so I create what I think will be desirable to others. After having received what I wanted, I released what was desirable to others. I was now in possession of what I "wanted," now that I was not alone. What I didn't see was that others had been doing the same thing!

This was the choice in childhood that I didn't know but now know. Did I ever grow up? I can't know others if I don't know myself. I can't love others if I don't love myself. The proper study of humankind is the study of oneself. We must be curious in what makes us do what we do. The essence of who we are is still there. We can feel it; we only need to look and allow compassion to replace what we don't know! In want or desire, I am self-centered in my fear, my judgment, and my confusion.

Want not!

# Chapter 17:
# Fear and Anticipation

## "Allowing fear prevents allowing."

### Fear

As my kids were growing up, I remember going through the house and having them turn off the lights in the rooms as they left. None of them could seem to do it. One day, as I was going through, I noticed something to my amazement. Daniel would turn off the TV and lights as he left the room. I had never told Daniel to do so. He had watched and listened. One day, I picked up Daniel to come visit with me in the place I was staying, and as we came in, I took him on a little tour. First, I showed him how I dropped the tailgate of my truck and told him how I got up in the morning to sit outside to meditate. I showed him the kitchen, the light switches, and different things about the house. As we started upstairs, I showed him some exposed wires. I told him not to touch them as they were live, and I showed him that they turned on the lights that illuminated the stairs. As he reached for them, I warned him again that it would really hurt him, and he backed off on his own. As we went into the main room, he needed to use the bathroom, so I took him in and showed him the toilet. He used it, and then we went to get something to eat. Upon returning, we went upstairs, and I use the exposed wires to turn on the lights. We ate, and then he said he needed to use the bathroom. I told him, "You know where it is," and he got up and used the bathroom after which we went to sleep for the night. When I got up the next morning, I was a little concerned about the things I told him and showed him the night before. The truck sat quite a distance from where we slept. As I went outside with my coffee, I went into concern in thought. I visualized Daniel waking up and not finding me in the room. I visualized him touching the wires, and I visualized his falling down the stairs. I started to get fearful. I jumped off the tailgate and started for the house, and then I stopped. I replayed the morning's events. I came downstairs to get my coffee. I turned on the bathroom lights. I awakened Daniel to let him know where I was going. I asked if he wanted to join me. I turned the lights on for the stairs and moved a box of books at the bottom, so he wouldn't have to shift sides and possibly touch the wires. I also turned on the entry lights, so he could see clearly. In realizing what I had done, I started to put the pieces together.

He knew that I turn the lights off when I leave, so with the lights on, he knew I was there. He knew about the wires, and he could see the stairs. He was 30 years old, and he was one smart cookie. If I stayed with my fears, as I had in the past, I would have found myself acting anxiously. More importantly, I would not have allowed Daniel the freedom to be who he is. A strange calm came over me that allowed me to sit and enjoy my coffee and write. This also gave him the freedom to explore and do as he felt, though he was so comfortable that he just slept. I, who at first was very uncomfortable in thinking and creating anxiety within myself, suddenly realized, once again, that my thoughts were creating something that was not! It turned out to be a very peaceful morning. That came through as he awakened on his own about eight o'clock.

I was able to see again how my thoughts where making me want to protect on him. Was I allowing him to be himself or wanting to protect him from my own fears? Was I preventing him from being himself in my thinking? Yes! Was I protecting him or me, and was I allowing him to express himself? Or, would I be holding him back in my fear? Thoughts and fears are not real until I act.

### Anticipation

Recently, Daniel was up to visit, and I went out to enjoy my coffee. I had not made any plans for what we would be doing, and I was anxious in anticipation of how we would spend the weekend.

Daniel, having limited speech, has learned to read or feel people when they are in thought. He was just waking up when I entered the room. I began talking with him, and he felt my anticipation. He began to put his hand in his mouth and was about to rage. I told him that this was Joe's house and that he couldn't do that here. I asked him what was happening. His response was, "Joe's house," then he removed his hand. It was the pause that I needed. He was telling me that my anticipation was not allowing. It felt like fear to him, and I was now aware of what I was allowing him to feel. This made me stop and not worry about what we would do. In that moment, he taught me to allow things to unfold. He gave me about two minutes as I let go of the anticipation. What could have been a chaotic day turned into a very peaceful weekend. Again, it was another reflection on, *What about me?* This was no different than my anticipation of what he might do to his baby brother or sister in our fears. Being simply loving was lost in, *I must have done something wrong,* within him.

Fear not!

# Chapter 18: Assumptions and Judgments

## "In judgment, there is only illusion and no allowing."

An assumption is nothing more than a judgment based on our thoughts of how we view ourselves. They connect us to our self-critics—this is how I see myself, so others must be thinking or doing the same. Knowing we all judge, we assume others judge our own thoughts. This is not necessarily true!

We also connect to fear in how we might be judged. In our reasoning, what is said or not said can no longer be true; it's only what we see in our thinking. In assumption and fear, if the truth is not spoken, assumption is now true in thought. As truth not spoken is a lie left to assumption.

In our relationships, as in childhood, our confusion is based in our own critiques or how we might be viewed by others in our fear of not wanting to be seen as different or not wanting to be alone or wanting to fit in. In this, we assume a new role: How should I reason so I'm not alone? This is where I left the love of myself to the judgment of myself in assumption. The assumed role is based on opinions, or the opinions of others were how I judged myself.

My first choice was to allow opinions as I didn't want to be seen as different or alone, and it was my choice. I allowed others to define me in my fear of their opinions. And it was a choice I was unaware of until I allowed myself time alone. What I didn't see was that I was resisting alone, and what I resisted persisted. It was in wanting that I became human or self-centered. I have allowed myself to love, and love is without self and needs nothing. It is allowing, as is the soul. This became my reflection: What about me is not loving?

Through this, I now know my speechless, autistic son.

Judge not!

# Chapter 19: Comparisons

## "Comparison is the denial of your being, to be who you are not."

This was the place in my new awareness where I started looking to others for my answers, where I saw myself as not OK or alone. I began to compare myself or rate myself through others' opinions and judgments that connected me with my self-critic. I could always see, in my opinion, that somebody else was doing better than me. Sports, school, money, life, works—you name it. There is always someone that is better or has more things.

School was the perfect place for ratings in comparison to others, and I was thus graded. In these comparisons, I saw clothes, hair, different groups, beliefs, races, religions, government—it was almost a form of brainwashing. Did I shift my thoughts to fit in? I did, to the point where I was being rewarded for doing better than others. This became a competition or challenge to get the reward for being better than someone else. This is how we are taught to compete—to be second place is not good enough. This conditioning, where we allow ourselves to be compared to others in someone else's opinion, becomes how we judge ourselves. It's also where we teach ourselves to hide for fear of how we will be judged in comparison to others. Compassion is not taught! A teacher could be a coach and ask students who are doing well to help others who are not doing so well. Being OK with who you are is not taught. We could teach those who know what they like to do and do it well; instead, it's the contrary. Everybody has to be the same, and they are graded on their sameness. What prevents me from allowing people to be different and help them build confidence in their differences—allowing them their purpose and passions?

All people are given abilities, but what keeps those abilities from being seen? Before I started coaching, I took my son to the games, and one of the rules of the games was that all players would play equal amounts of time. Because of the lack of volunteers for coaching, most of the coaches were parents and had their kids on their own teams. Their kids wanted to play certain positions, so their parents placed them in those positions whether or not they had the talent.

This caused a variety of issues, such as favoritism. The parents placed their children in those positions because the children wanted to stand out in the eyes of the parents and gain status in the eyes of their friends, teammates, other team players, and girls. To the parents, it was, *Look how special I am. Do you see my child?* To the child, it was, *I'm special. I can do as I want.*

It also caused oppression. The other players on the team were not given equal time because they were not considered as good enough. Yet, they were there to learn to play something they enjoyed, to be a part of the team, and to have fun. I was able to talk to parents during and after the games. They sacrificed time and money to get their children into the games. They would leave disappointed because their children had not played at all, or if so, very little.

When I signed up for coaching, we went through the process of choosing teams. I didn't know the players, so I listened to the other coaches, who had agendas of their own. Most of the players I wound up with were considered to be less talented. I didn't care whether they were talented or not as I had my own agenda. When we gathered for the first practice, I explained what I wanted. I had a set of rules. First, we were there to have fun. Second, I wouldn't tolerate anyone making fun of anyone. Third, those players who were good at something would help the other players learn to be better. Forth, if they wanted a position, they had to earn it. This one applied to James as well. I also explained to them that everyone would play the same amount of time. I pointed out that, if the other teams could see a weak player, they would attempt to take advantage of him, so it would be to their advantage to help him get better.

Daniel, being the coach's son, automatically had an advantage. He was as one of the players on the bench, and they treated him with favoritism. Through those years, he had a blast. He had a lot of friends. James, on the other hand, was disturbed at first because he didn't get the position he wanted even though he was the coach's son. He thought he should get the position without having to earn it. His mother was also angry as he would come home and complain that I wouldn't give him the position he wanted. She felt that, because I was the coach, he should have it. This made no difference to me. I still felt he should have to earn it. I would not show favoritism toward anyone. It was an even playing field, and for him, there were bumps. He finally got his position, as did many others. During our practices, what could have been competition became a companionship of helping each other be better than they thought they could be.

During the games, they had the joy of watching their fellow players achieve. They shared the excitement and the disappointments and continued to help each other as they could see their own weaknesses. Most of all, they were having fun! They shared little things. They could see some of their friends didn't have the right equipment because they couldn't afford it, so the extras were shared. Old skates were given to them—wheels and bearings, sticks, helmets, gloves, and whatever was needed. It was during these times that I often thought about the other kids who couldn't play because they didn't have money. How many kids will never do what they love because their parents don't have the money to help them? Whether it is for sports, science, mechanics, building, art, music, and so on, through greed, there is incredible waste. As I'm writing, a movie comes to mind called *The Rocket Man*—a must see!

When it came to the playoffs, our team took first place. Yes, they wanted to win and had learned how to do it. This team was considered to have some of the worst players. Over the years, I had many teams, and all of them had the same rules. All of them finished first or second. I saw kids who were on drugs, and it wasn't supposed to be allowed, but I felt nobody needed to know. Many kids had home issues, many had very little, but for a little while, they had each other! Something I hadn't noticed at the time was that Daniel's rages were at a minimum. He was accepted as he was. He was being allowed to be himself.

For me, after having learned the basics, school became a lesson in redundancy. To me, it was all the same over and over again with no point. I became bored. I was becoming lost in the insanity of confusion, fear, and judgment. In my final year at school, I was called into the principal's office with my mother. The principal said, "I can see you are a smart young man. What seems to be the problem?" I didn't know. I was confused, became angry, and began crying. I vented through my confusion. As I look back now, I can see what the issue was. I felt I was being asked to be the same as everyone else. And I wasn't. No one is! We all have different talents, different gifts, different ways that are covered up in wanting to be the same. Where was the joy in knowing we are all different?

The school system knows there is something missing. The parents know. There are more and more kids being homeschooled, and yet we know there is a need for interaction with people. A team literally works together through their strengths and weaknesses to be better. The coach places those individuals in positions according to their strengths that will best serve the team. If the individual doesn't care for his or her position, it's up to the team to help make him or her stronger. This is only my opinion, and maybe we need to take time to allow for individuality and stop grading our achievements according to someone else.

A team is only as strong as its weakest link.

How will the world become a team?

When will we allow for our differences?

A team becomes great when it loses the, *What about me?*

I wonder. Could it be that the autistic being knows that he or she is different and that he or she will never be the same as anyone else? Does this allow them to focus on and pursue their purposes? Could it be that these beings are able to use their minds without fear or want and become savants? We find parents going out of their way to encourage them in their gifts and talents regardless of the outcomes, financial or otherwise. Could it be they are living and we're not? Maybe that's why they seem to be so joyful. Could it be?

# Chapter 20: Emotions and Judgment

## "Emotion is felt, and we choose not to feel in judgment."

Emotions are the most direct link to who we are. Our inner selves sense and feel our environment. Yet, in this sensing and feeling that started in childhood, we now connect thoughts to feeling as we've become more aware. In this new awareness, feeling gives way to confusion; we notice that we are now in a world where we view ourselves as not the same as others. This is where the protector takes over—reasoning, thought, the mind.

We begin to allow our environment in the mind to form this idea of not the same as or being alone. We begin to connect to the assumed judgment or self-critic in fear of how we might be viewed by others and ourselves. We don't want to be alone or seen as different, so we begin to hide. We start seeking the approval of others, not realizing we are not approving of our own being—paradox! And the story of who we think we need to be begins.

The differences between men and women are set up early in childhood. We assume the roles or respond to the judgments of those who are in our lives early on. A male is supposed to hide his emotions away and not be emotional. A female is allowed to be emotional, yet she's not allowed to be strong. Both connect with fear of the assumed opinion or judgment of others. We begin to create what is approved of even if it is separate from what we feel. All this is from not wanting to be alone, and all have created this in this same way. It is how we keep reliving our childhoods. Not knowing who we are, we then begin to create who we think we need to be.

The mind is now in control, and we begin to become emotional in our thoughts. None of these thoughts are real, but we choose to live them. Yet, there is a deep-seated feeling that something is missing. Who is missing is the being that you are, lost in confusion, wanting to be seen and heard and not knowing how. For me, I had to release the thought of alone and allow. I had to release the thoughts of assumed opinions and judgments of others and allow. I had to release the thoughts of fear and allow. I had to release the thoughts of want or don't want and allow. I had to realize that thoughts are not real until I act. The energy, soul, being, or chi that we all are has no thought. It is pure innocence or love as God! Everything to this point has been a judgment created in the mind. That is not real. Nothing unreal exists unless we choose to create from thought. In biblical terms, it is said that the body is a temple. Part of the temple is the mind. What we are, though, is not the mind. This might explain the after-death experiences of people who say that they saw everything happening and they experienced great peace. Or, they were out of their mind! It's said that the mind is a terrible thing to waste; in these parts, it has been wasted! We can all have peace when we choose to stay out of our minds. We are not living; we're surviving.

# Chapter 21:
# Jealousy and Envy

## "The child in everyone knows more and is now hiding the soul"

Jealousy and envy are not the natural state of our being. I was unaware of how they were created. In the uncovering of the different parts of my self-creation, I journeyed deeper into the rabbit hole. I found this too was also created in the first awareness. In childhood, my view of the world around me was that everyone seemed to know more than I did. My view was that everyone was better than me. In that view, I was not OK. I had no love of me. It was where I started to hide in the fear of not being approved of. Nobody else seemed to see this judgment. I was self-critical, and everything became my fault. This is where Daniel lives. He knows he's different, and because of his difference, he assumes the responsibility for his being different, causing issues in others and, for him, confusion as to what he's doing wrong—just as I did.

The idea that everyone is better than me began very early on in my childhood. I was not aware of the subtle shift in my newfound tool the mind, which began creating a protector from the realization that I was not the same. This view—that everyone is better than me—is the same view, realized in jealousy and envy, carried through adulthood in relationships, possessions, and beliefs. The cycle of self-creation begins through wanting, fear, and judgment. In the beginning, in this new awareness, we lost our being to the confusion of how to be. This alone, wanting, fear, and self-criticism, when looked at, are a cycle that feeds on itself. In not choosing to look at our self-creation, we choose not to see our self-created suffering. We are reliving our childhood creation. Instead, we choose to want to know what makes a person do what they do instead of looking at what makes us do what we do. I have always known that I cannot lie. I've also known that

I'm not here to harm anyone. What I did not know was the illusion created in my mind to survive, where I lied to answer the question, *Who am I?* I will not convict myself for what I did not know. And I cannot convict someone for what they do not know. Love is allowing! Who you are is allowing, yet it's complicated in thought or in the mind.

We are all on the same journey, allowing people to be who they are, and doing what is needed for their growth is essential. Not knowing what others need and accepting prevents jealousy and is allowing. I can still love them and myself knowing that I can't be everything to everyone.

## Soul, Being, Energy, Chi, Yin-Yang

As we dismiss our souls to reasoning, there is a feeling. We've learned alone—the one thing we are and that we don't want to be. So, we begin to create in reasoning. Most will not say who we are. Most will not say you're OK. Most will not say you don't have to create yourself. Most will not say it's OK to feel. Instead, most will say you have to be something or do something.

Most of us go searching for ourselves in others' opinions to fit into what we consider a safe place—most popular clothing styles, haircuts, peer pressure, church, government—not knowing all are divided in opinion.

And yet, aren't we attracted to those who know their own purpose, those who can be themselves, those who march to their own drum, those who follow their own feelings to help outcasts like the young boy, with his mother's help, giving out blankets to the homeless, those who dare to not listen to the fear of others' opinions and follow their inner voices that lead them to their passions, their gifts, their talents, and true joy?

We assume in our judgment that others know more than we do. After a while, we notice inconsistencies in others that aren't true because, like us, they too aren't aware of who they are. They, like us, created who they think they need to be—a thought creation.

We're thinking of ways to be like everyone else—that's the first confusion or doubt. The subtlety is felt as we leave our soul to reasoning. This reason uses words fear, and criticism and creates in thought who we need to be. Step into the fear means to step into the feeling that we've attached to a thought.

Feeling things doesn't happen often in this life, and all the while, we know something's missing. Death draws closer, and we begin to stop wanting to be a part of something and begin to see that our lives could've been different. When we don't try to be the same, we're beginning to live!

We choose to prevent ourselves from living through fear, criticism, and doubt based on others who don't know what they're creating. We are getting ready to leave this behind, and we will return to who we are—soul, being, energy, chi.

No thought, no reasoning, God within—life is ours no one else's. No one can live it for you, and it is your choice to stop making everyone else more important.

Do we know we're killing each other? Do we know we are oppressing others and ourselves for our own reasons? Do we know who we are?

We are souls attempting life together; we are still alone and will soon leave alone. What does it look like to allow each other life? Have we become so chaotic in the fear of being alone that we are not living? Are we not allowing others to live? If so, we are already dead. We chose not to see. There is only this moment; the future is guaranteed to no one. Will you start living your purpose?

Now, I have to share the place I had to go after my awakening in 2010 to affirm that I was not losing my mind. I was losing the illusion created in it!

# Chapter 22: Compassion and Love

## "No fear allows."

It's funny if think about it. Give this one a moment. True love is without self, true compassion is without self, allowing is without, and self-humbleness is without self. If we are not in all of these, are we not self-centered? What is referred to today as love is about self-wanting from the place of thinking alone. The paradox is in today's way of thinking about love. When true love is given, the person is viewed as needy, less than, foolish, or someone to be taken advantage of. To allow oneself to be in this place is to literally step out of the box and be the fool.

To release such judgmental thoughts is to come back to one's soul. To be strong, allowing, and compassionate for oneself and others is walking a courageous path. The key concept to understand is that strength is humble. I usually know what's needed, yet because of fear, confusion, doubt in my judgment, or from some form of wanting, I've oppressed myself and others. To be humble is to step out of self-centeredness created in fear, confusion, doubt, judgment, or want and allow, which takes strength.

Compassion is the ability to place oneself in others' shoes, and compassion is only one part of love. Most of compassion comes through experience, or I should say, we don't really know until we experience. Through the experiences we have, we make mistakes. It's critical or judgmental to say we sinned; it is to know that which we didn't know.

How do you really know anything until you experience it? After having lived the experience, we may be able to share without fear, wanting, or criticism, and step out of the above and be humble and compassionate. Through our experiences, we know, and to not share is oppressive to ourselves and others. To know our experiences is how we get to where we are now. We can't know until we experience, and to express those experiences without fear, without guilt, without wanting to be OK in other people's eyes is being humble and allowing. How does it feel to know you didn't do anything wrong? All experiences are needed to get you to where you are now.

To allow each soul to live its purpose is difficult as we have not been allowing of our own souls, which have no thought of self. Knowing how our self-concepts were created with our thoughts in the mind allows us to be compassionate when we see others doing the same. They just don't know it yet.

# Chapter 23:

# The Division

As I went through the process of looking within to see how I think, many things became very clear. Maybe it's time for a new perspective. This will not speak of religion and will speak about what I've come to know as religion. Although most religions are based on the belief that there is a Creator, most say, "Look within, and know thyself." The Bible does this as well. I have read the Bible many times from cover to cover; I finally threw it aside because I knew I was missing something.

Upon my divorce, Martha gave me a new Bible, the King James Version, at which point I told her that I would probably never look at it again. After my awakening in 2010—yes, you guessed it—I started looking at the Bible again, this time as an affirmation of what I was now seeing. I asked, *Am I losing my mind?* The answer was, *Yes, my mind creation.* Each time an insight came through, I was guided to words written in the Bible. The words were telling me that I was OK, to keep going. I was now literally being led on the journey that Jesus suggested we take—within. "Let go, and let God (You)." The words reminded me of how my soul became lost. I was now seeing the Bible as an owner's manual or a reminder of how to reconnect with one's soul. To me, it describes how we've become divided within— how the family is divided, how the church is divided, how the government is divided. I was continually being led to Genesis, where it all began, especially Genesis 1: 6: It describes our first awareness of who we are and how we separated from our souls.

In the beginning, a family unit is described. Man was created to tend the garden. Woman was created as a "help meet." This word has been misconstrued and interpreted as a being one who is less than. *Help meet* actually means to help one another meet God within, to meet with that unconditional love that is in each of our souls. It means that, when we care enough about each other, we choose to look at the untruths we have created with our minds.

Today, the wife is misconstrued as a possession by law, and we are to be caretakers of the earth. Adam, after being punished by God in his new knowledge, names his partner because she was the mother of all living. It is stated that very way in Genesis 4: 20, not the mother of all man. It appears to me that Eve was named after Eve, the mother of all life. Perhaps this is where my confusion began; we aren't sure who we are. What really caught my eye was Genesis 3: 22: "And the Lord God said, behold the man is become as one of us." Doesn't this seem to be telling us who we are? Jesus spoke these words again in John 10: 34: "Is it not written in your law, I said ye are Gods?' " If this is confusing, change the word *God* to *Creator.* As we all know, we create our own suffering and our own happiness. Luke 17: 21 says, "The kingdom of God is within you!" John 14: 20 says, "At that day ye (you) shall know that I am in my father, and ye (you) in me, and I in you." Could this trinity actually be saying one soul and that the division of three began in our thought? I for one feel separated from God and Jesus when I hear *trinity.* And when I hear "I am in you, and you are in me, and we are in God." As it is stated, I feel a peace, a togetherness, a knowing that I am with God, and we can create together. If we are all one, as it states, then with "the faith of a mustard seed," nothing is impossible. If the seed is faith and as our awareness of this faith gradually starts small and grows into the knowing of who we truly are in Jesus, in God, imagine the mountains we could move. Imagine the joy we could create for the greater good of our own souls and the greater good of all. Another example appears in John 14: 6–7. Verse 6 we've all heard, and check out the line that follows: "I am the way, the truth, and the life: No man cometh unto the father, but by me. Verse 7 reads, "If ye had known me, ye should've known my father also: And from hence-forth, ye know him and have seen him." Now, we have seen the Father, and we see what Jesus's words mean.

If the prophets and their words are so good, what is the need for Jesus? He was to be an example—to speak the words for us, to show us how to begin the journey inside. He gives us the greatest commandment in Matthew: 22–37, 38, 39, and 40: "Thou shalt love the lord thy (your, you, soul) God with all thy heart, and with all thy soul, and with all thy mind (not your created mind and to recreate your mind)." This is the first and greatest commandment. And the second is like unto it, "Thou shalt love thy neighbor as thyself. On these two commandments, hang all the law and the prophets."

Matthew: 23–13 says, "But woe unto you, scribes and Pharisees (preachers and pastors), hypocrites! For ye shut up the kingdom of heaven against men; for ye neither go in yourselves, neither suffer ye them that are entering to go in." Funny, it seems we are still being asked to look outside to find God and Jesus when God and Jesus both are saying look within.

I have to go back to Genesis and something I missed. Genesis 1: 26 says "And God said, let us make man in our image, after our likeness." Genesis 1: 27 continues, "So God created man in his own image, in the image of God created he him; male and female created he them." Curious how *him* refers to male and female. To me, the implication is a male God and a female Goddess.

Genesis 2: 7 says, "And the Lord God formed man of the dust of the ground, and breathed into his nostrils the breath of life; and man became a living soul." Genesis 5: 2 adds that "Male and female created he them; and blessed them, and called their name Adam, in the day when they were created." We are souls; we see opposites and opposites attract, male and female. This was meant.

The key word here is *soul* or *being*. This changes after Adam and Eve eat from the tree of knowledge. And this is where the fear, want, blame, judgment, and game begin. It is the first awareness. "We did die to our soul being who we are." Adam, in his guilt and fear of the assumed judgment, didn't want to be found out by God, so he spoke these words, first blaming God and then the woman.

Genesis 3: 12 says, "The woman whom thou gavest to be with me, she gave me of the tree, and I did eat." I wonder, didn't he have a choice? Yes, yet he was a child with a childlike curiosity represented in the serpent. God didn't judge; he only punished.

Daniel's nakedness made me think of Adam and Eve. They had no shame. Neither does Daniel. The innocence he has I can see. He wanted to be like everyone else, yet he couldn't. This brought constant confusion. All this was a reflection point that led me back to the beginning—Adam's shame and confusion, Eve's shame and confusion. Adam and Eve's eating of the apple was simple child's curiosity. Life should be this simple. Their curiosity gave way to mind thoughts of shame, guilt, and confusion. This was the death spoken of. Who we are is now what allows the mind creation.

There are many more references in the Bible as to this divide spoken of by Jesus—too many to mention—and it is that our thoughts are deceiving our souls. The body is the house of the soul, and part of the body is the mind. The body and mind are our physical equipment, yet who we are is energy or soul. Thus, we are twofold beings. This was the piece I was shown in my awakening in 2010. I saw how I was divided. I knew me, and saw my thoughts, which were not I!

So, what of the Ten Commandments? They are similar to the words spoken by our parents. It's no different than when we tell a child not to put his or her finger in a fire. Then, if the parents walk away, what usually happens? Some children touch the fire. After that, they know; they had to experience to know. It is the same with the tree of knowledge and with the Ten Commandments. God is love (allowing), and He is all knowing. If we think for one minute God doesn't know what we do...well... Life wasn't meant to be so hard.

What of Cain and Abel? I see now that this is a description or metaphor for sibling rivalry, how in our wanting to appear better in our parents' eyes, we connect with jealousy and envy. We choose that we are not good enough, and it is how we kill ourselves with our own opinions, our own judgments. And we keep on living this way. It becomes a competition. To allow ourselves to know this, and see our children doing the same thing, could we connect with compassion and help our children see what they're doing to themselves? Forgive them, for they know not what to do. And forgive us, as we didn't know either. God did allow Cain to live, just as we would our children as parents.

The great flood—I asked myself what the reasoning in this would be. Then, I was shown. In Genesis 6: 5, "God saw that the wickedness of man was great in the earth, and that every imagination of the thoughts of his heart was only evil continually." A thought is not real until I act, making it real.

To act from a place without self is allowing and is love.

Regarding the tower of Babel, Genesis 11: 4 says, "And they said, go to, let us build us a city and a tower, whose top may reach unto heaven;" this was shown once again as they were attempting to find heaven outside. In Jesus's words, the kingdom of heaven is within you. Look within. Like a poor marksman, I kept missing the target of these words. The target is you and I. The words were spoken to allow us to reconnect with our souls with allowing, compassion, humbleness, and selflessness. I had allowed myself to fall into opinion. To allow each other our passions is our souls' purpose; we feel it. What is it to gain the whole world and lose our souls? We all feel it! We can change our minds, our perspectives, and our opinions. The words spoken by Jesus and God were crucified with Jesus.

# Chapter 24:
# Graph

### The Epilogue

My journey down the rabbit hole brought me full circle back to my soul. I saw how, as a child, my fearful thoughts of being separate and alone allowed my mind to act as my protector. I saw how, as an adult, I still operated from that survival mind-set. Although I got smarter in getting what I thought I wanted, I still felt something was missing. I realized I had dismissed my soul, which wants nothing and allows everything. As the Bible says, "The man who thinks himself something, when he is really nothing, deceives himself." Once I reconnected to my soul, I was able to connect to Daniel on a soul level as well. I could see how his thoughts of being different and alone were creating the same suffering for him. I was able to convey to him that he had done nothing wrong. All experiences and mistakes are necessary to learn what we don't know. I now use my mind rather than my mind using me.

I created the following graph to help me visualize where I am: in my mind (the right triangle) or in my soul (the left triangle.) Notice how want, fear, and judgment feed on each other in the right triangle. If I am in one, I am in all three in my thoughts. If I am having an issue, all I have to do is look at the right triangle in order to see where I am stuck. Remember, a thought is not real until it is acted upon. I can choose to change my thought or mind perspective and operate from the left triangle. I can reprogram the computer to take control of my mind rather than my mind controlling me.

Where are you?

### The Epilogue

I had allowed my mind in childhood to become my protector, in order to survive. What I didn't know was that I was still living the child. The right triangle is the child reasoning in self or "thought." I BECAME SMARTER in that survival, but I still "felt" something missing. I had dismissed my "soul." Who I am! (Left triangle) to become Who I am not! (Right triangle.) The brain was still reacting as the protector. From what? Others' opinions in their survival and creating the same way.

The man who thinks himself something, when he is really nothing, deceives himself. Notice how in the right triangle, Want, Fear, and Judgment work on each other, or feed on each other. It was a cycle. I was stuck. And if I am in one, I am in all three in thought. And a thought is not real until I act on it, or live the thought. If I am having an issue, all I have to do is look at the right triangle to realize in what part I am stuck. Then I can "choose" to change my "Thought or Mind or Perspective," and reprogram the computer. I'm taking control of my mind. It is no longer controlling me.

Where are "YOU"?

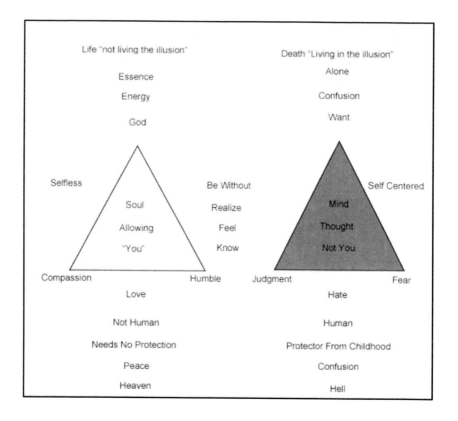

So begins
Your
Journey
Down
The Rabbit
Hole . . .

Good luck, happy wandering.
Don't give up.
Stay with it.
Take two aspirin and call me in the morning.
He he oh ah . . .
They're coming to take me away, oh he oh ah . . .
L.O.L.

### Truth

This is the truth. As I have allowed myself to sit after 2010, many things have become clear. I have allowed myself to become silent as my son and stay alone in my thoughts. I sit in the morning quiet in meditation, and as I meditate, there sits before me a tree I call the lollipop tree. This big, round tree sits in front of two pine trees that rise above the lollipop tree approximately 20 feet. One day I walked in meditation around the lollipop tree and found that the pine tree is actually one tree that has separated and rose as two, yet it is one tree.

This pine tree is a beautiful metaphor of what I had become. Early in childhood, I realized that I seemed to see and feel differently than everyone around me. That left me with the thought that I was different or not the same and alone. This was the beginning of my creation of my fear of different, and it was where I allowed my mind, in the equipment given me, to take control.

This is where the tree begins to split into two parts. It is where I left my being, or energy that I am, to become what I thought I needed to be, so I would not be seen. I began watching others in how they behaved and began criticizing myself in the view that everyone around me knew themselves. I needed the approval of others, and I became competitive for this approval to say to myself that I was OK. I was really not OK in my own eyes. This was the beginning of the paradox of allowing. I allowed others to rent space in my head. My soul continued to grow as I did, only split from me, yet with me, allowing me to experience what I needed to experience. The tree may never grow back together; we can when we remember.

I did not allow myself to be different because of my own fear, my own judgment, my own thinking. Everyone was better than me, and I became envious of others. This happened in childhood, and is happening in our children. No one did this to me. It was my choice. And no one did this to you. I didn't know what I know now, and now, I can change the program in my mind. What we consider to be right or wrong is our own choice, and to allow ourselves to understand the mistakes we make help us see that we couldn't know until we had the experience. We must get up and try again in our new awareness.

None of us wants to harm anyone. To realize how we oppressed ourselves is to be in compassion for others, knowing they have to experience life in their own way. To start using the mind without the need to defend is to step out of survival and live and allow others their experiences. Then, it's no longer a battle of the minds but a connection to all on a level of allowing.

Fear, criticism, judgment, or want are the programs of the mind set up in childhood, and we have become smarter in this redundancy. What is written is only a reminder of what you already know. All the experiences of childhood we just don't remember, and I will not convict myself for what I have forgotten, as I would be making myself accountable in my own self-critic.

To stay in allowing, I have to dump the criticism, fear, and wants or my mind's creations in defense. They are self- or mind-centered. Who we are looking for and the peace we seek have become lost, and we only need to remember how.

Everything and everyone has a purpose. Our purpose is the passion that we feel. To live our passion has become lost in opinion and thought—that you have to be this or that or that you have to be a certain way to get what you want. Yet, we know it's not about getting; it's about giving. We all want to help, yet have we allowed our passion, our purpose? Or, have we oppressed our passion to be like everyone else. We feel our passion, and in living our passion, there is great joy. A sharing of that passion allows others to allow their passion in seeing your joy. In the fear of alone is how we hide our passion. Allow your passion—you will see there are others with similar passions and that you are not alone. The anger and frustration in this world comes from our own oppression. We've allowed our own oppression through fear. Allow your passion in your purpose, and live, then allow others to live!

*And the journey continues...*